Canon Charles Martin, Headmaster of St. Albans School, Washington, D.C., 1949-1977.

Letters from a Headmaster's Study 1949—1977

by Charles Martin

Edited by Louise D. Piazza

Second Edition, Revised and Expanded

UNIVERSITY PRESS OF AMERICA

LANHAM • NEW YORK • LONDON

Revised and Expanded, Second Edition

University Press of America,® Inc.

4720 Boston Way
Lanham, MD 20706

3 Henrietta Street
London WC2E 8LU England

Printed in the United States of America

ISBN (Perfect): 0-8191-5387-7
ISBN (Cloth): 0-8191-5386-9

Cover design by Anne Masters

All University Press of America books are produced on acid-free paper which exceeds the minimum standards set by the National Historical Publications and Records Commission.

DEDICATION

To St. Albans School from which I have learned so much and which I love so much.

Preface to the Second Edition

These letters were written to members of the St. Albans School family with no thought that they might one day be collected and published. Indeed, the first edition (published in 1961) would not have been save for the insistence of members of the School family and a visit from the original publisher, Oxford University Press.

This revised, expanded second edition also would not have been possible save for a visit from Dr. John Chamberlain, president of the St. Albans Alumni Association (1982–84). Dr. Chamberlain reported that the Association would like to have not only the letters of the first edition republished but would also like to publish those that I wrote during my subsequent years at the School. I demurred politely at his suggestion because many of the letters appear to me to be dated. However, Dr. Chamberlain spoke forcefully in behalf of the project, and whatever the alumni of the School ask of me I do!

Fortunately, the Alumni Association provided the project with an excellent editor, Louise Piazza. She fed me the edited letters in clusters with appropriate comments. A few were embarrassing to me, a few seemed too preachy, and a few belonged to the past. On the whole, though, I didn't mind rereading them.

In fact, I enjoyed some of the letters. Each letter, growing out of the common life of the School and addressing the needs of the moment, is an entity in itself. Many readers may prefer, as I think I would, to skip about in the book and read according to subject matter and interest. I hope that these letters may be of some assistance to you in understanding and living with your young people.

I can say with conviction that I enjoyed my association with St. Albans School and that I have learned much both from the boys and from their parents. To all of the School family, I am deeply grateful.

Charles Martin

Charles Martin

June 1985

Acknowledgments

I would like to express my appreciation to the following individuals for their support, guidance, encouragement, and suggestions in the preparation of these letters for publication. Fran Johnson, Director of Development at St. Albans School, first conceived the idea for the book; she initiated the project and supported all facets of its completion. Members of the St. Albans Development Office staff have all been most helpful, rendering assistance in many ways. From the outset, the St. Albans Alumni Association Executive Board has given its wholehearted support to this project and has provided financial assistance for the editorial work.

In addition to those mentioned, my thanks go to Joy Hammers for her meticulous typing of the final draft and for her editorial suggestions; to those who wrote new prayers for the book; to Paul Piazza for his editorial input; to the St. Albans library staff for their help in researching facts; and to Mary Ellen Holbrook, Charles Martin's secretary, for her gracious help.

Finally, I would like to express my gratitude to the members of the St. Albans faculty and staff and to its current headmaster Mark Mullin—all of whom have given time, effort, encouragement, and support in the completion of this undertaking.

The Editor

Table of Contents

Selected Excerpts

Foreword

by
JOHN C. DAVIS

John C. Davis served as Assistant Headmaster of St. Albans School under Canon Martin, as college advisor, and as a teacher.

When Charles Martin first visited St. Albans School, he petted my cat, Pancho, and she bit him. This was not a discriminatory act on her part — she bit everyone who intruded upon her comfort. But Canon Martin may have felt the act symbolic. In fact, had I been Canon Martin coming to St. Albans School in 1949 to assume the position of headmaster (succeeding the Reverend Albert Hawley Lucas), I would probably have turned around and gone back to Vermont. I am sure that, in those early two or three years as headmaster, he must have felt as though he were an alien in an unfamiliar environment.

None of the faculty, of course, liked the change of headmasters (or any change, for that matter). To me his arrival represented a transition similar to that of leaving college for the larger world of limited economic independence. Mr. Lucas had done everything himself, had known all that was going on, and — as far as he could — had ordained the future. We were now on our own.

Mr. Lucas had extended his parochial and pastoral ministries far beyond those of the School, though not beyond scriptural injunction. He had written every St. Albans boy who served in the military; he had even sent letters of sympathy, support, and advice to people only remotely connected with the School, many of whom he did not know personally. This sort of projection of the St. Albans parish into a broader world was a prediction of the path that the School was destined to follow during Canon Martin's twenty-eight-year headmastership.

Charles Martin probably saw that his task — other than to keep St. Albans running smoothly — was to decentralize and to delegate. The School from 1929 to 1949 had been so much a reflection of Mr. Lucas's personality that it was evident — however much the faculty may have hoped for the contrary — that such a single-handed mode of operation could no longer persist.

Whether we knew it or not, Charles Martin was the right man to take on the task of decentralization of responsibility; both the conditions and the time were ripe. Washington, D.C., with its old bureaucracy and social structure, had grown with the Second World War. If the School were to retain its place, it too had to branch out and expand. To have dealt in the older way with such a large number of students would have been impossible.

Expansion of the School structure was slow and sometimes went unnoticed. Over the years, however, the administrative tasks of admission, college placement, routine counseling, departmental organization, alumni relations, fund-raising, representation in national associations, faculty development, curricular and extracurricular expansion, and even publicity — all were created from the nucleus of Mr. Lucas's one-man and highly dramatic activity.

Charles Martin had been left the legacy of a fine faculty, charismatic men of varied talents, all endowed with the quality of projecting not only their subject matter but also their personalities into the minds of their students. These great teachers, who moved on into Canon Martin's headmastership with him, taught with a flair for communication and a coruscation of personality that engaged the able, amused the dilatory, and dragged along the unwilling with the inevitability of fate. Over all these, Canon Martin did not merely preside; he ruled. If he lacked the boisterous physical presence of his predecessor, he was of equal moral impressiveness, for behind his amiability and his willingness to concede in minor matters, lay the same determination to make the School a first-rate example of the Divine Will, while his unyielding Puritan ethic channeled the School's operation. Fundamentally, then, there was little difference in the School's philosophy — as secular educationalists call moral purpose — between the rule of Mr. Lucas and the reign of Canon Martin.

Born in Philadelphia (that city of quiet distinction), Charles Samuel Martin was St. Albans School's fourth headmaster. Before coming to the School, he had taught at the Episcopal Academy in Philadelphia and had served for seven years as a parish priest in Vermont before embarking upon his headmastership of the larger parish of St. Albans School. He carried on a life-long love affair with the Green Mountain State, so much so that a faculty member, noting that one of the headmaster's favorite hymns was being sung for the third time in one week, called it the Vermont National Anthem.

For a headmaster of a school like St. Albans, such a swarming parish of boys and their families could only increase and multiply. Not only did the School's size grow from 364 to 530 during his tenure, but wives, children, and friends were added to the number who came to him — with increasing frequency — to seek advice, help, information, consolation, or simple hand-holding. Nor was anyone turned away. A part-time secretary once looked ruefully at the dictation that had magically expanded over a holiday weekend, remarking, "He's the only man I know of who ever answered a thank-you note."

Through this network of ghostly counsel — spiritual support — Canon Martin encouraged his ideals of education. Starting with the practical problems at hand — academic difficulties of the students, marital problems of the parents, personal loss — he moved into the spiritual realm of character formation, reconciliation, and compassionate healing. Always, he was aware of the priority of God's jobs over those of Mammon, and if Mammon's were demanding too much time, so much the worse for them. "To the mischief with it!" was his harsh judgment upon them.

Charles Martin was not an educational theorist. Although

in his time he saw that St. Albans School was among the first to introduce an outdoor survival program; social service in the ghetto; courses in Russian, African studies and penology; or the use of media as the educational message, he was eminently pragmatic. He wasted little time on talk, moved at once to personal action, and on one occasion (though over 60) rappelled down a forty-foot wall to demonstrate to worried mothers that it was a safe activity. (They were not convinced.) When his harried administrators thought they had completed the job at hand and had the program working, Charlie Martin was off stirring up educational anthills in another area, and wanting to send students to work in the back country of Tanzania or in the Richmond penitentiary. There was no rest for anybody, least of all for him — nor was rest considered desirable.

Long before politicians had rediscovered the work ethic, Charles Martin was preaching it. In the midst of the late-60's youth revolution, when so much individual convenience was disguised as moral message, he grumbled publicly about "what they thought was so wrong with the Puritan work ethic." In those troubled times, when deans and heads of academic institutions were being held hostage in their own offices, Charles Martin was busily anticipating student demands, organizing their reasonable educational expectations into a program, and, in essence, staying miles ahead of them. Imaginative foresight was one of his greatest gifts.

An important reason for the milder effect of student protest at St. Albans was Canon Martin's own philosophy of administration, which was simply to try the new wherever possible and to change, and change, and change, and change yet again. So when students reached the barricades on the other side, they usually found Canon Martin helping them over, and a crowd of agreeable if not always agreeing faculty smiling behind him to implement a change that went far beyond student imagination.

Charles Martin's administration at St. Albans was marked by development of the School structure, enlargement of the concept of the School community and its social responsibility, and by growing awareness of the increased role of non-academic education in the broad practice of instruction. An innovator, he saw that the present need not be enshrined externally in an unchanging carapace, however jeweled, for the moment of the contemporary rapidly becomes the educational past. For him the future of education was like the old comic strip showing the frankfurter tied to a stick, which in turn was tied to the dog's back, so that the animal chased the future hot dog forever. Restless, never satisfied, creating new goals as he pursued his high ideals, Charles Martin made a good School great, and a high ideal more capable of realization.

The web of human influences, seemingly tangled yet patterned, produces lives that are mysterious, though perhaps they would be explicable to us were we to know the intimate design of their weaving. A disorderly or disordered influence may produce a disordered web, like that of a spider that has been given dexedrine sulfate.

A great headmaster such as Charles Martin has the power to share in the orderly weaving of a life marvelously patterned in its form, with center and purpose, like Jung's center of an integrated person — aware both of his destiny and destination. And the fragile, complex human personality — deep, intricate, and diverse — deserves no less than his total honesty and dedication.

At the bedrock of his character, Charles Martin considered the humanity of man important, but not so important as its divine ingredient. When he said once that he was not trying to get students into Harvard but into the Kingdom of Heaven and a bright lad muttered audibly, "When is the Director of Admissions going to visit," Charles Martin only smiled. Perhaps he knew.

Notes from the Editor

Compiling and editing the parent letters of Charles Martin has not been an easy task; indeed, the headmaster emeritus would be suspicious were I to say it had been. From him I have learned much — not only about the challenge of raising children, but also about coping with the problems one encounters in daily living. Though I have not always agreed with his advice, I have been encouraged and uplifted. I have come to know and admire the writer of these letters, and in the process I have gained great respect for his common sense, his eloquence, his sense of humor, his enduring Christian values, and his pertinacity in the face of change and crisis.

More than a decade ago, when my husband and I took up residence in the St. Albans dormitory (where we served for several years as dorm parents), Canon Martin helped me carry a side chair up a flight of steps. Through these letters, he has helped me up other, steeper stairs in my life. It is my hope that as you read the letters — either separately or in their entirety — you will gain insight into or assistance with a particular problem in your own life or that of your children. In his letter entitled "Blizzard" Charles Martin writes, "There will always be flights of stairs to be climbed. Our hearts, minds, and bodies need to be ready for them."

From the sheer volume of letters and the multitude of subjects addressed during his twenty-eight-year headmastership, one might deduce that letter writing came naturally to Charles Martin. Such was not the case. In fact, he labored long over each letter, wrestled with each turn of phrase. Sometimes, pressed with work, he was forced to send out a letter he had written years earlier. On one such occasion he stated, "I explained to parents who asked me to write a letter about college placement ("Admission to College") that letters do not come easily to me. I said that I could not, at this time, write such a letter. I have settled on the next best thing — a letter I wrote twelve years ago."

And there was always the ubiquitous red pen of Ferdinand Ruge — legendary St. Albans English master, whose name is synonymous with grammatical and rhetorical excellence — to contend with. Charles Martin routinely submitted a draft of each letter to Mr. Ruge for editorial review. The letter would come back to him marked with "as much red ink as the paper of a Fourth Former." He and Mr. Ruge would then minutely discuss each correction. In most cases, Canon Martin acquiesced to his colleague's recommendations. Theirs was a working partnership: one based upon mutual respect and affection. It is not insignificant in the scheme of things that Mr. Ruge passed away just one month before Charles Martin retired as headmaster.

Charles Martin wrote these letters to parents and friends of the School because of a deep, abiding conviction that he spoke to a community united in a common Christian purpose. In his words, "I have always wished that our St. Albans family could come together in one place at one time and that we might sit down and have a meeting of the minds and of the spirit. Such a meeting being hardly possible, I try in these letters from the headmaster's study to meet with you, and I feel closer to you all."

A sense of Christian purpose *is* everywhere evident in these letters. Charles Martin is, first, a preacher — a man of God. Making biblical parallels, reminding readers of events in the Christian calendar, using a New Testament parable to drive home a lesson, offering Lenten injunctions, he constantly appeals to our spiritual natures. He believes that "a man is made of one piece," and that to neglect any aspect of life — especially the religious — is "to lead to impoverishment of the spirit and to make all life the poorer for it."

The early letters, in particular, are heavily laden with religious content and with what Canon Martin — reading over these letters for republication — termed "too much piety and preaching." "My gosh, what an awful lot of preachment," he remarked to me. "Too much preaching, too much drivenness, too much certainty, not enough wisdom." He explained that, thirty years before, the School family had been composed of two-thirds churchgoing Episcopalians and that he could never write today in the pious form in which he had then written. "Times have changed and Martin has changed," he concluded.

Writing with warmth, sincerity, and depth of feeling from his own experience, he uses anecdotes culled from family life, from events in his friends' lives, from conversations with colleagues, from world affairs. Whenever possible, he teaches through the everyday occurrence: the boy who could not "find" himself, the young master troubled by the turn of current events, the parent "at the end of his rope." These down-to-earth examples, laced with humor and good sense, are what cause the reader to listen and laugh; to sympathize and reflect; and, finally, to understand. Even though an issue may be one that we have met many times before, Charles Martin has the ability to jog us out of our preconceived notions, to shed new light on an old subject, to retell a human truth in a fresh way. Leading us to reconsider, he inspires us to tackle a seemingly insurmountable problem anew.

Charles Martin met the issues of the moment — both secular and religious — head-on, not shrinking from the painful or controversial. He loved to be in the thick of things. Whether the subject at hand was bad manners, bulldogs, student protest, or Nixon's resignation, he focused his considerable energies upon it, looked at it from all sides, and suggested ways to deal with it. In some cases he was straightforwardly unequivocal. "My own attitude toward the use of marijuana is clear and unambiguous. The use of 'pot' is wrong." He was equally firm about all boys being required to take athletics, about their not being absent from school because of snow or sickness, about their mandatory attendance at chapel. While the firmness might at times have seemed unyielding and Puritanical to his charges, the man lived what he spoke. And although abiding by such rules might have been tough, there was security in knowing where the headmaster stood on issues.

Yet there were other instances in which he was not so uncompromising. Like all of us, Charles Martin was sometimes angry, often uncertain, frequently troubled by what he witnessed occurring in the School and in the world. And he said so, using these letters as a forum. The letters show him grappling with weighty matters that subsequently changed the course of history. What becomes apparent as we read through the letters chronologically is the tremendous educational, social, technological, and political upheaval that took place during his tenure — Korea, Sputnik, man's first moon walk, campus revolt, Vietnam.

As the winds of change swept through the School in the late '60s and early '70s, the headmaster emeritus adjusted; he mellowed. Far from damning or ignoring the new and unconventional, he went out to meet it. The letter "There is a Season" shows him seeking to understand the viewpoint of the "hippies." In the face of student unrest and the use of illegal drugs, he tried repeatedly to communicate his beliefs to parents and students. He called in experts, reviewed and evaluated the evidence, presented both sides, distilled his views.

Still, at the core of his being, his values remained unshaken and unshakable. While the length of a boy's hair might be permitted to change, the boy was still expected to dress neatly. Old values might be revised, but they ought not be discarded.

A certain charming dated quality graces some of the early letters. It is amusing to note how the outward trappings of teenage social life have changed. We can chuckle at a car being referred to as an automobile. Our young people *seem* to be so much more sophisticated and worldly-wise than they were in the '50s — yet these anachronisms render the letters no less meaningful. Charles Martin's advice certainly has a timeless appeal. Nodding appreciatively, we come to realize that there is very little new under the sun. Reflecting the fashions and prevailing morality of the times in which they were written, the letters still speak forcefully to us today. The difficulties and rewards of child rearing have not really changed so very much.

Underlying all his counsel in the letters is Charles Martin's concern with the process of growth from youth to maturity, that journey toward wholeness undertaken by us all. As its hallmarks, that process has humility, wisdom, and love. Happily, the former headmaster has not stopped writing. In a letter to the editor addressing an article about the joys and pains of teaching *(The Washington Post,* October 30, 1983), he wrote, "Occasionally the teacher recognizes that he has touched a life and made it richer, perhaps even made it whole. And what satisfaction can compare with that?"

These letters *will* touch your lives — your minds and your hearts — in some way. Of that I am sure. The following words, written by Charles Martin in 1974, serve as a fitting benediction to the counsel contained in this collection: "Parents, my friends, love your children, trust them, have confidence in them, let them go. They will find their way, and it will often be a better way than we could have planned for them."

— Louise D. Piazza

Our Father, who has set a restlessness in our hearts, and made us seekers after that which we can never fully find: Keep us at tasks too hard for us, that we may be driven to Thee for strength. Deliver us from fretfulness and self-pity; make us sure of the goal we cannot see, and of the hidden good in the world. Save us from ourselves, and show us a vision of a world made new. And may thy Spirit of peace enlighten our minds, until all life shall glow with new meaning and new purpose; through Jesus Christ our Lord. Amen.

*Henry Sylvester Nash**

**A Boy's Prayer Book*, compiled by John Wallace Suter, Greenwich, Connecticut, Seabury Press, 1957, pp. 50-51.

I

Arrival

September 15, 1949

Dear Friends,

My family and I arrived at St. Albans on September 1, receiving a very cordial welcome from Mr. Heartfield* and several faculty and staff members, all of whom have been most helpful in settling us in our new home. For a while I was sure that order could never emerge from the chaos, but it has. Now I have the opportunity to do what I have wanted to do ever since my arrival — write to you.

I am most grateful to members of the St. Albans faculty and staff who have been at the School over the summer. Evidence of their work is everywhere apparent. The buildings fairly glow. As I sit at my desk, slowly seeking to absorb some of the detail involved in running this School, I realize how effectively they have met the ever-present problems of School life during the summer.

---

* Mr. Maurice K. Heartfield served as Chairman of the St. Albans Board of Governors from 1949 to 1950. His son, Maurice K. Heartfield, Jr., is St. Albans' Administrator.

Mr. Lucas** stopped by for a moment on his way to perform the wedding ceremony of an alumnus. It is heartening, indeed, to know that one's predecessor will be in the background, ready to give the advice so needed. Each hour that I am here I see more clearly the imprint of Mr. Lucas's legacy and personality. Although I can never fill his shoes, I pray I may be as effective as he.

It is good to be at St. Albans. I look forward to the new year and the opportunity of sharing with you the upbringing of your sons. When next you are at the School, I shall be grateful if you will stop in to see me. Will you please remember me to your boys? We are looking forward to welcoming them on opening day.

Faithfully yours,

Charles Martin

** Canon Albert Hawley Lucas served as Headmaster of St. Albans School from 1929 to 1949.

O God, whose son was the Teacher of men,
Grant that all teachers may work in His spirit,
Earnestly, patiently, and humbly,
To nurture their pupils in accordance with Thy wisdom and Thy purpose;
Through Him who taught that men might be saved, Jesus Christ our Lord. Amen.

*Ferdinand Ruge**

---

*English master at St. Albans School from 1933-1977; Assistant Headmaster of the Upper School from 1960-1968.

II

First Impressions

December 21, 1949

Dear Friends,

During the first few weeks of school, so many new faces, ideas, and situations were before me that all was a jumble. After three months, however, I begin to have some definite impressions of our School.

It has been much more fun to be at St. Albans than I had anticipated. I was not sure how I would enjoy returning to school work, for it had been seven years since I left the Episcopal Academy in Philadelphia. The world changes greatly in seven years, and so does one's self.

Your sons are fine lads. After the Senior Prom, even though it was two o'clock in the morning, Mrs. Martin and I sat for a while talking of the group of fine-looking boys and girls. We spoke of their poise, manners, attitudes; we spoke of how much we enjoyed being with them. The boys are well behaved — I don't mean incipient angels, for they are quite human. Yet they are courteous, purposeful, and interesting. It is good to be with them.

Among our faculty are some of the finest masters I have ever known. It is a great group. Last year our academic record was excellent, and I doff my hat to the gentlemen responsible for it.

Mr. Lucas looks in every few weeks for just a moment. He darts in to say hello and then is on his way. I am always conscious that he who has meant so much to the School and who stands ready and eager to help is always behind the scenes. The deep impress of his personality upon the School will not easily be forgotten.

I like to think of boys, faculty, parents, alumni, as a family. When any one member of the family does something, the whole is interested and, to a degree, joins in. At a football game, not only the team but all of us participate. Only as we are all cheering, sharing in the game, does the team do its best. Next year we shall add a new section to our grandstand — for I know we will need it.

In the months I have been here I have met many alumni. Living in Washington, I have learned already that almost everyone comes to this city sooner or later. They may come to attend a convention, to visit a government agency, or to do some sightseeing, but come they do, sometime or other. When you do come to Washington — or if you are one of the many already here — please drop by and say hello. The whole Martin family will be glad to see you.

This letter will reach you just before Christmas. I hope that you give and receive lots of gifts, that your Christmas tree be big and bright, that your children be many and merry, and that this old family festival be the most joyous you have known. Most of all, I wish that the Spirit of the Child who came into a family and made it and all life holy be born anew in your hearts, and that you and yours come to know that peace which passeth understanding. God bless you!

Faithfully yours,

Charles Martin

Seeing we also are compassed about with so great a cloud of witnesses, let us lay aside every weight, and the sin which doth so easily beset us, and let us run with patience the race that is set before us, looking unto Jesus the author and finisher of our faith.

*Hebrews XII: 1, 2**

*Epistle for All Saints Day, *Book of Common Prayer.*

III

Korea: Time of Tension, Tragedy

January 31, 1951

Dear Friends,

The subject of Korea brings a dark cloud to my consciousness. None of us, not even those who live in Washington, can predict the outcome of the present conflict. Naturally, we are all gravely concerned over the tension, the tragedy of these times. Not the least of our concern is their effect upon our boys. Our nation's initial uncertainty over policy has made it difficult to determine what those effects will be. We at St. Albans have been watching, ready to move as soon as the fog has cleared. Although the situation is far from clear, certain trends are evident. It is about these trends I write.

We have been keeping in close touch with the Civilian Defense Office and other informed services, ready to act as directed or as events dictate. We will enter on a program of training only as outlined by the Defense Office. However, in all kinds of special ways we have prepared our School — masters, boys, buildings — for whatever may come. While none of us wishes to believe that war is imminent (and I am one who strenuously believes that war need not and must not be), I want you to know we are conscious of the kind of world in which we live. At the moment life appears grim. As we look at war's imminence and at the potential for annihilation by the H-bomb, the future, indeed, seems far from promising. Certainly, it is neither the kind of world nor the kind of future we would wish for our young people. What does the possibility of war mean to our older boys? How will it affect their college careers? Universal military training is a certainty. At what exact age training will begin and which boys will be deferred, Congress will shortly determine. While colleges have been completely in the dark as to the effect of the draft upon their student bodies, certain facts are now emerging. Most colleges will hold summer sessions beginning in June; there will be February graduations; general acceleration will soon make it possible for a boy to complete part of his higher education before he is drafted. These facts may alter the plans of some members of our graduating class. Eventually, St. Albans may have to institute changes. In any case, we shall be prepared.

I know how troubled you as parents feel at the thought of some of our boys going into the service. I also know something of the upset our young men must feel. The attitude of our boys, however, is reassuring. Their morale is strong. These youngsters, God forgive us, have lived all their lives through crises, wars, and threats of wars. They take the present tension in their stride and go steadily on doing their job and doing it well. I do not imply that all of them are placid and unconcerned, for who could live today, call himself a man, and not be sensitive to the fearsomeness of the times? Boys do reflect our uncertainties and our worries, but on the whole they plough their furrows with remarkable detachment and thoroughness. We must do likewise. Sufficient unto the day is the evil thereof.

The number of reservists among our new teachers has me concerned; the draft has already cost us one of our new masters. Among our alumni, an ever-increasing number of our younger men are being called into the armed forces. Almost daily someone comes in to say, "Did you hear that Jones '39 or Smith '40 has entered the service? Paradoxically, I want to hear such news, and yet I don't. It seems to be beyond belief that we should be seeing our young men entering the service again. But as long as any of our alumni goes off, I shall want to be informed about it. I will try to write letters to those in the armed forces; they will be remembered in our prayers in the Little Sanctuary. I am mailing to our alumni in the service a prayer book as well as a war cross, both of which will serve to identify them with St. Albans and with the Church.

Even as I write this letter, war in all its tragedy has come to us. I just received a telephone call that Munro Magruder, Class of '44, was killed in action in Korea on September 3. Pray for Munro; pray for all of our boys, and pray the good Lord that we who are parents and schoolmasters may yet have the wisdom and the righteousness to build a world where such sacrifice need not be required.

Being a parson, I just can't help preaching. I believe that it is only as we find a security and a strength in One who is in a sense outside and beyond our times, that we can give to our children, who are so sensitive to our moods and attitudes, the ordered life, the sense of purpose, and the feeling of security we would have them know. Whenever — as in these times — I grow very troubled and depressed, the meaning of Christ on the cross sweeps through my mind. Even though wrong, evil, and sin may seem to triumph and bring goodness to the scaffold, God's will must ultimately be done, and right and goodness must triumph.

Faithfully yours,

Charles Martin

We thank Thee, O God, for the wonders of Your creation; for the energy sources within and above our earth that supply our daily needs, all of which we take for granted.

Help us to develop and use the technology supplied to us to sustain life, to improve life, and to bind closer Your children of every nation. Grant us the wisdom to understand Your gifts and their intended use through Your personal guidance.

Through Jesus Christ, our Lord, Amen.

*Earl R. Arnds**

*Earl "Doc" Arnds taught mathematics at St. Albans and served in many other capacities at the School from 1935 to 1978. At one time he taught a course in auto mechanics.

IV

Automobiles

November 4, 1953

Dear Friends,

At the moment, automobiles are very much on my mind. This morning I called into my study a boy who had been speeding through the Close.* At lunch, I spoke to the boys about driving to and from football games, reminding them I wanted to see all of them on Monday morning — in one piece.

All of us — parents and schoolmasters alike — are concerned about cars. Some of us dread the day when our son reaches sixteen and craves a driver's license or claims having a car as a right. We are all anxious when our sons are out driving or being driven. Those of us with vivid imaginations spend some troubled moments whenever our son is not in the house at precisely the moment we think he should be. Yet it is of no use to hope that our boy will not request a license. He will, and he ought to have one. It is also useless to worry when he is out driving or to nag him continually about safe driving habits. Automobiles are very much with us, both as a bane and as a blessing, and every driver needs to know how to drive carefully and well. Our job as parents and

* The Close: the precincts of the Washington Cathedral, which include St. Albans School.

schoolmasters is to instill a sense of responsibility about the use of cars. If that responsibility is not accepted, or if it is violated, then we should take action — decisive action.

We are currently investigating offering a driving course at St. Albans. Perhaps it seems natural to include such a course in our curriculum. In the past I have tended to be unsympathetic towards such courses on the grounds that schools are taking on more and more of the responsibilities of living and failing to do that special job for which they exist — that of providing sound academic training. Schools are often called upon to teach everything from habits of cleanliness to good manners, until their primary reasons for being are forgotten or neglected. If we cannot fit such a course into our curriculum, I strongly urge each of you to arrange for your son to take a driving course at a driver-training school. He will learn much, both in theory and practice, that you as a parent cannot give him.

Next, let's set the record straight about whether your son really needs a car. For some parents, the problem is solved by a factor that brooks no argument — finances. For others, the answer is not so easy. Your son ought to have a car if he is ready for it and needs it. We all know how we can rationalize ourselves into believing we need what we want: we must recognize this tendency both in ourselves and in our sons. As I see it, a car is needed in the following instances: if it is otherwise awkward for you to get your son to school; if family strain can be eased; if life is made more comfortable or time gained for more fruitful living. Your son ought not, however, to have a car if it is a plain luxury. Although he might earn enough money to buy a car, I would be opposed simply to giving him one. He ought never to have a car because "everyone else has one." Everyone doesn't have a car. Fewer than a quarter of our Sixth Formers have one, including those to whom it is a genuine necessity for transportation. A larger number are occasionally permitted to drive to school in their parents' cars. By far the great majority of students are permitted to use the family car(s) only for special occasions. Do not buy your boy a car until you can afford it, until you think he can handle it well, or until you think for some good reason he should have one.

Now a word about the kind of car. In writing this, I don't want to step on anyone's toes, although I wouldn't hesitate to do so if I thought I were right. Fortunately, I think I have arrived at that age when I realize I am sometimes wrong! I would hesitate to buy my son one of the fancy new foreign sports cars. I doubt that they are as safe on our American roads as they are on English or continental roads, and I doubt that they offer as much protection as do conventional American cars. I must confess I would like to have such an automobile. These cars look quite attractive, and I would like to zip, even zoom, along the road. But I would not buy one for myself or for my children, not only because I do not trust myself or them, but also because I can't control other drivers on the road.

Even as I write this I realize you can't take all the danger out of life. Many things are more important than being safe. We are too much concerned with security these days. Life must be measured in terms of quality, not quantity. For a boy who has that rare common sense and good judgment bestowed on so few of us, perhaps a sports car or convertible is justified—for the rest of us, no. Now let's consider the other end of the spectrum — jalopies. If your youngster is mechanically minded and likes to tear down and rebuild rather than to drive, fine. But don't trust the life of your son and his friends to anything less than the safest car modern industry can provide.

When your son does have the right car and has learned to drive carefully, don't worry about him too obviously or unnecessarily; don't be a backseat driver; and, finally, don't nag him. On the other hand, don't allow your boy to drive with someone who is not responsible. A car in the hands of an immature or irresponsible driver is a violently dangerous weapon not only to the driver but also to the public.

The best that we parents can do in life is to provide our children with the finest equipment possible in the way of inner resources and then encourage them to meet life on their own terms. We can be on the sidelines, always ready to offer assistance as requested or to interfere on those rare occasions when we must. However, to interfere continually, to convey even unconsciously our worries and anxieties, is to be less than a good parent. I don't mean to say that I wouldn't clamp down hard when necessary. If your son does not handle a car responsibly, I am all for taking it away or for taking any other necessary action. Few teenagers are all-wise; most need some guidance — even guidance that is in the spirit of "the rod."

We do, however, need to avoid communicating anxiety and tension to our offspring. Thus, the rules for driving I have been speaking about will be kept not through any nagging or unpleasant insistence on our part, but through a spirit that is in us and communicates itself to our young people. We shall know that spirit and our young people will know it as we and they come into the presence of Him who died that all might have life and have it more abundantly.

Faithfully yours,

Charles Martin

O God, who hath given us the joy and the responsibility of children,

Enable us, we beseech thee:

To know our boys as they really are,

To impose the discipline and to grant the freedom they need for their growth,

To help them grow in understanding and strength, that they may know what things are good and hold to them,

To help them overcome fears and anxieties and grow in confidence, that they may enjoy their work and their relationships with others;

And we beseech Thee to guide, protect, and strengthen them that they may continue to grow in wisdom and stature and in favor with Thee and all people; through Jesus Christ our Lord. Amen.

*Craig Eder**

*The Reverend Craig Eder served as Chaplain of St. Albans School from 1953 to 1973. Currently he is involved in the parish ministry.

V

Parties and Social Behavior

December 9, 1953

Dear Friends,

A complaint came to me this past week about the misbehavior of a group of St. Albans boys at a party. Troubled, I investigated. As so often happens, a core of truth was embedded in a wildly exaggerated report. However, our boys *had* been at fault, so I called them into my study to hear their side of the story.

A number of them out for an evening without any planned activity had been attracted by an open house party. It was a huge affair with boys and girls from many schools milling around, talking and eating, all coming and going as they pleased. No adults were in evidence; no program had been planned. So our boys ate and made merry. One bit of horseplay led to another until things became so rowdy that our boys, concerned about their own behavior and bored with the party, left. Although they had been neither destructive nor malicious, they had engaged in some pranks and mischief. Their behavior had upset the party and spoiled a good time for many, themselves included.

As I spoke to the boys, I tried to point out that they had been thoughtless and inconsiderate. I stressed that, at a party, their job was not to wait to be entertained but to entertain, not to lounge in the corner or camp by the food but to join in the fun and make the party a success — all in good spirit and with a sense of responsibility. If things began to get out of hand, their job was to leave.

Because they are good boys, they realized that their foolhardiness had done more to harm the School's reputation for gentlemanly, courteous behavior in a single evening than they could have done to improve it through a year of good conduct. Apologizing to me, they promised better behavior, having gained some concrete ideas about avoiding similar incidents in the future. I hope they will henceforth represent the School more favorably.

Such episodes, I suppose, are natural to the growing-up process; even so, I wish they could be avoided. We have a wonderful group of boys at St. Albans. I want everyone to know them for what they really are — at school, at home, in other people's homes; in fact, wherever they are.

Much more than adults, our young people need to know how to conduct themselves in social situations. They need to know what time their parties will begin and end, what parties they may or may not attend, whether or not to accept alcohol, with whom they may or may not ride in an automobile, and what time they must be home. They do not want to seem different from their contemporaries; at the same time, they want to seem like the adults they aspire to be. While they may not readily admit it, young people want, welcome, and need our guidance and support.

Thus, I should like to comment about parents' roles in acting as hosts and hostesses at a young people's party. If your son is to give a party, Mother and Dad ought to be on hand for it. You are the ultimate hosts. Welcome the guests; make them feel at home. Don't intrude on the party, but be discreetly, inconspicuously present. As guests leave, accept their goodnights and thanks.

Enjoyable parties rarely occur spontaneously; rather, they require careful thought and advance preparation. A party is a big undertaking for everyone concerned — children and parents — much too big a job for many of us to tackle. The best the average one among us can manage is a modest party that includes only boys and girls known to our children and excludes uninvited friends who appear hopefully on our doorstep, eager to "crash" the party. To me, an open house party signifies trouble; it is an invitation to disorder and wild behavior. I do not believe that a large group of young people — many of whom do not know each other — can enjoy a good time. I know that parents are often uncertain about how to manage their own children, let alone a horde of other people's children.

It is not always easy for us to know the answer in any given situation — social or otherwise. This is especially true when we hear that "everyone else does" or that "times have changed since you were young." Times have indeed changed, and many people act as we ourselves would not. Social conventions vary; even fundamental moral principles are not shared by everyone. Yet it is our responsibility as parents to offer guidance and give strong support. It has been my experience that indecision on the part of parents is worse than severe or even lenient decision. Young people need to know certainty — what is and is not to be. They respect parents who know what kind of behavior is expected and who hold to their convictions.

Certainty in all situations is, I realize, difficult to achieve. It is much easier for me to advise parents than to perform the job myself. I simply wish to pass on my experience. I know that a master cannot teach effectively without a sense of certainty and authority in him that engenders respect. Likewise, a parent needs to project a sense of authority that communicates itself to a child. I do not mean to say that one should be harshly autocratic or unduly arbitrary. One must always be considerate and understanding, but he must also act as a parent, giving the support of strong judgment that arises from conviction.

What hour should John arrive home? It depends on his age, his destination, and his plans. A definite time should be set; if an unavoidable delay occurs, John should telephone his parents. A 15- or 16-year-old attending an early movie should come home directly afterwards. If he attends a party, a reasonable time should be allowed for him to take his date home and return home himself. My heart rejoices when a boy who boards at School asks me for permission to attend a party that is to end at 11:00 or 11:30. I always respond with a grin and say, "That sounds like the kind of party I'm in favor of. Get along, my son. I shall see you in half an hour after it is over."

If there is to be a formal dance and it is a very special occasion, perhaps it is reasonable to go to the Hot Shoppe or a small party at someone's house afterwards; these occasions, however, should be rare — perhaps two or three times a year. When this permission is granted, a boy ought not be allowed to attend a party after a party.

To aid both young people and their parents in coping with the problems of creating a good social life, the Association of Independent Schools of Greater Washington has prepared a set of helpful guiding principles. They read as follows:

GUIDING PRINCIPLES IN BOY-GIRL SOCIAL LIFE

1. Social activities of students should be confined to weekends and holidays and should end at a reasonable hour.

2. When students entertain, parents should be present or available at all times.

3. "Party crashing" should not be tolerated.

4. Parents and students should have a common understanding as to the time a student should return home from a social function.

5. Parents and students should have a common understanding as to where and with whom time is to be spent.

6. The practice of "parties after parties" should be discouraged.

7. The common courtesies, such as prompt acceptance (or regrets) of invitations and appropriate dress at social functions, should be taught and their practice insisted upon.

8. Since schools do not permit the use of any alcoholic drinks at their social functions nor allow any student who gives evidence of their use before these functions to participate in them, parents should follow this practice in any party held in their home or under their sponsorship.

9. Since parents have a moral as well as a legal responsibility for those whom their sons and daughters may have in their

cars, they should see to it that their children are trained to be, and continue to be, considerate and courteous drivers, with a keen sense of responsibility for the safety of their passengers and others.

These guiding principles are no panacea, nor are they all that I would have them be. However, they do make clear that we — parents, boys, schoolmasters — share the responsibility of bringing about that kind of social life we all deem desirable. Moreover, these principles indicate directions in which we all can act. Most important, they indicate the spirit in which we want to act and the ends toward which we want consistently to aim — consideration and thoughtfulness for one another, common courtesy, and gentlemanliness. The spirit of these principles can make a better world of even our little world.

Finally, the raising of children involves a lot of fun and a lot of pain, whether it has to do with parties, drinking, or the opposite sex, but it is also the greatest privilege we can have in life. We shall do it well or poorly, depending upon the quality of life we ourselves have been able to develop, the way we are able to learn, the humility of heart that helps us to recognize we do not have all the answers and that we can learn from each other and occasionally from our children, through whom God has been known to speak even to parents.

Faithfully yours,

Charles Martin

O God, give me the courage to change what can be changed, the serenity to accept what cannot be changed, and the wisdom to know one from the other.

Reinhold Niebuhr

VI

The Process of Growth

June 1954

Dear Friends,

I have just completed five years at St. Albans. It doesn't seem that long until I look back, and then events and faces crowd upon one another, and five years seems too short a time to have encompassed them all. It is strange to note the events that stand out in my mind.

I can envision a boy making a speech in the dining room. Although I don't remember the substance of his talk, I do remember the battle he fought and won against shyness, the fears and nervousness he overcame. I knew his agony and his triumph. Then there was a lad, soft and selfish. I can see him yet. He graduated after — not blood — but certainly sweat, toil, and tears. I knew with him the satisfaction that comes from reaping the rewards of sustained effort.

Students like these stand out amidst other memories. A swirl of events, those that make up the exciting life of our times and of living in the capital city, claim my attention. Reminiscing among such occurrences as the Korean War, elections, the McCarthy hearings, bombs, and the race question is not always pleasant. Through these memories run a deep uneasiness, a somber heaviness, the continual threat of nuclear bombs. How educated and yet how stupid can we be! We uncover the secrets of life seemingly but to destroy life.

And yet I must confess that I am one of those fortunate souls who by temperament enjoy the conflicts and the battles of life. I like to pit myself against forces, be in the thick of things, take a licking, and occasionally achieve a victory. Just to be alive is good to me. On the other hand, I doubt that I would get much satisfaction or peace of mind unless I felt that — in some small way — I was cooperating with the purposes of Him through whom all life becomes worthwhile, Jesus Christ our Lord.

However, I must also confess that, not infrequently, I find it difficult staying on top of things. Being easily stirred by a host of interests and enthusiasms, I often assume more responsibilities and activities than I should. Then come frustrations, a sense of pressure, and irritability. Not being able to lay aside obligations easily, I am often forced to reexamine the use to which I am putting myself and my time. I always try to do my reexamining in the Lord's presence — if you will, I say my prayers.

When I pray, no special magic takes place, and I don't suppose I am ever transformed, but I am helped. For one thing, I relax; then I see things more clearly. Problems that seemed insoluble, that I couldn't untangle, issues that appeared huge and troublesome, take on new and manageable dimensions. Perhaps most important, I realize that I can't do all things. I know again what always ought to be in my consciousness — that this is God's world, not mine. The sermon or address I have been worrying about will come in its own time, with a wisdom and a spirit that are absent when I labor with anxiety. As I reexamine and learn to husband my time more wisely, life takes on a new perspective and new strength — sometimes, I think, even the strength of the Lord. At any rate, I carry on more effectively than I otherwise would.

Headmasters are often regarded by those who do not know them as curious, remote creatures who wield, in their own limited domain, unlimited power — ogres who keep boys in fear and trembling; despots who command masters to come and go; unbending disciplinarians who make unreasonable demands on young people. Nonsense! Headmasters are poor creatures subject to the control of overfilled appointment books, of individuals moving in all directions simultaneously, to cries of help here, a summons there, an emergency everywhere.

I do not mean to suggest that headmasters don't enjoy the hurly-burly of their lives. They do, and they somehow prosper and grow old with dignity. But I do want to disabuse all men of any notion that headmasters are individuals of free will, possessors of arbitrarily used powers. Such is not the case. Rather, they are servants of all — men whose privilege it is to minister as well as to administer, to teach some, and to help others. And that is as it should be.

You may well ask why one would elect such an arduous way of life. Or, to carry the question a step further, why, with only one life to spend, would any man choose to minister and to teach? That is like asking a mother why she loves her children or a boy why he loves to run. They are made that way. A master teaches because he wants to, because something deep within him impels him to that calling. He is held inescapably by the whole exciting process of growth and development and also by the limitless nature of human potential.

I visited a class at the beginning of the school year. The first boy I saw was Johnny, and I hardly recognized him. He had grown three inches over the summer. I marveled, but not for long, because sitting beside him was Bill. Although Bill had not grown much taller, he had changed greatly. His voice showed it, but, even more, his new poise and manner proclaimed his growth. Beside him were Tom and Henry as well as all the other Toms and Henrys who make up a school. Each had grown in some way. I came away awed. Each year boys undergo the same process, but I never become accustomed to it. I forever marvel at the mystery of growth in boys.

A man teaches because he is grateful for new life and for the opportunity of sharing in its joys and in its pains, because he loves the touch of mind meeting mind, and, finally, because he stands in awe before the mystery of human growth.

There is another side of the coin to such joy and satisfaction, and that is the recognition of one's failings and weaknesses. To learn from our mistakes is a difficult lesson for us all, even for the most conscientious among us. This lesson was once painfully brought home to me through my treatment of a purebred cocker spaniel of which I was very proud. I spent much time with that dog, training him to perform all sorts of tricks. He could beg, roll over, and walk on his hind legs. I delighted in showing him off to my friends. But the poor pup became neurotic. He started behaving disagreeably, snapping at my family and occasionally having a fit. After much doctoring, the vet kept him for a while and then, with my consent, gave him to a family in the country. Though I never saw the dog again, I heard that he prospered with his new family.

What had I done wrong? I had driven the poor animal to distraction. So eager had I been to have him perform for my own pleasure that I had never allowed him to enjoy being a puppy or even a real dog. However, all was not lost. The dog did get a good home, and he helped me to be both a better parent and teacher. I began to learn that one has to allow a living creature to grow in its own way. You can't drive; you can't force; you can't shape too much. Though this seems an elementary lesson, it is a very important one.

It is easy for us to seek to relive through our children the glories of the past or to experience through them the glory we never knew but to which we always aspired. When a boy fails to live up to our expectations, even though it may not be his fault, we are disappointed. Sometimes we are able to conceal our disappointment and accept the youngster as he is. Other times the hurt is so great that we show our displeasure, not so much in what we say as in our attitude, and our boys, who are more sensitive than we appreciate, are thus damaged.

Every master has seen a boy reduced to tears because he didn't succeed in athletics or in academics — not so much because of what it meant to him but because of what it meant to his parents. We have all seen grades suffer and personalities change when a lad became unhappy as a result of a parent's disappointment at his failure.

I don't mean to suggest that the average boy is a poor unfortunate who suffers from complexes induced by the ambitions of insensitive parents. Such is not the case. A youngster is a tough animal who will experience some rough times — one who will grow well either because of or in spite of us. We needn't worry ourselves unduly about complexes. Most youngsters are too sturdy and their powers of adjustment too good for that. But the whole growing-up process will be greatly facilitated if we can learn to accept our boy for what he is.

To do so is no easy job. First of all, it is difficult to see our boy in a true light. We may see him as we think he is — an image of the ideal rather than the real. We may grow irritated at what we deem to be his lack of growth in a certain area. Although we do not intend to misshape our sons, we fail to see. We fail to accept.

Acceptance — difficult though it is — is not enough. We must love a boy for what he is. To love a child who is vastly different from what we had always desired him to be is not a simple task. And it is never easy — even under the best conditions — to love that strange creature, our child, during that stormy period when his personality is changing drastically and a new independent self is emerging — adolescence. Yet in order to grow well, a child must know and feel love for himself.

I don't mean to imply that we can never be satisfied with our children as they are, nor should we allow them to think that we are. We must always be seeking to aid them to become their finest selves, striving to help them overcome weaknesses, especially those we recognize as having come straight from us — or perhaps from "the other side of the family." That means holding them to their best, having their reach exceed their grasp.

Our job at St. Albans, then, is infinitely more complex than teaching boys the three R's, holding them to high academic standards, and preparing them for college. We must always consider the whole boy. A lad will not grow mentally, will not achieve the academic success his abilities permit, unless he grows in all phases of his life. In order to grow well, he has to be understood for what he is and nurtured in the direction his potential will permit. Our task, put in religious terms, is to nurture each boy into the fullness of manhood God has purposed for him.

Such a purpose may appear to be an impossible task, but who has ever said that taking a human being from a state of complete helplessness and guiding him into becoming a whole person is easy. Being a good parent is not easy. The wiser ones among us realize that we need all the help we can get, not only from each other, but also from Him who is patient, understanding, and wise beyond any human being.

Faithfully yours,

Charles Martin

At work in his study — mid-1950's.

May the spirit of the Christ Child be born anew in you this Christmas and bring you joy and good works.

And may the lion and the lamb lie down together that we all may know peace. Amen.

Charles Martin

VII

Christmas

December 18, 1954

Dear Friends,

I have just come from visiting the new son of one of our alumni. It was a moving experience, and for no unusual reason. At the hospital I found the mother of the baby, with friends about her bed, looking wonderfully well and with a loveliness and gentleness that could have graced a queen. I offered her my congratulations rather diffidently, visited for a few moments with those present; then the proud father took possession of me.

We went off to visit the nursery. A fine little boy, not unlike other babies I have seen, was brought to the nursery window. He was wrinkled and red and yawning, with a quantity of hair that had not yet known a comb. There was a moment of silence, a silence heavy with awe. Then we all spoke at once. I don't recall what we said, but joyousness and congratulations were shared among us. I looked at the father. He was no longer the boy nor even the young man I had known. There was a new dignity about him, a new maturity, a new life. What had once been a boy or a mere man was now a father.

Returning to the mother's room, we gave her our congratulations and spoke of the wonder of her small son. After a few minutes I said a prayer of thanksgiving for the baby's arrival and then, leaving a small gift — an offering — I went my way.

I walked out of the hospital thinking of the wonder and mystery of it all, remembering the birth of my own first child, musing about babies, mothers, and fathers. When a new baby comes into the world, a new life is born in the form of a child, and a new life is born in people. I thought of the dignity and strength born in the father, of the new grace and gentleness born in the mother. As I walked more lightly, I marveled at the new life born in me.

In all reverence, the first Christmas was like that, and every Christmas is like that. A Jewish maiden knew that a child was to be born unto her. Like every mother who ever lived, she knew that her child would be no ordinary child. Yet this holy Mother was convinced that her babe was to be the Son of the Most High, the Messiah Himself. In her heart God assured her of that. She and her betrothed Joseph had to wend their way to Jerusalem. Like so many in her day, and for that matter in any day, she had neither the security of a home nor a comfortable place in which to bring forth her child. He was delivered in the only place available — a stable.

Shepherds came to visit the new baby, wrinkled, red, and wonderful. They saw the mother in the midst of the stable, lovely, radiant — a queen. They saw Joseph, strong with a newfound dignity. They visited; they offered gifts; they left, with the angels singing in their hearts of peace and good will.

Some there were who were wiser than the rest; they saw in the signs of the times, in the very heavens themselves, that this child who had been born in a stable was no ordinary child, that He was the Son of God whose birth had been foretold by the prophets — the long-expected Messiah. Like the shepherds, these wise men came, offered their gifts, and went away awed by the mystery of creation, by God's bringing new life, even His life, into the world. And the new joy that was in them lighted their way.

For two thousand years men have been visiting that Christ Child, that Family, and new life is always born in them. Peoples have come and gone, nations have risen and fallen, great leaders have ruled and been forgotten. Change has taken place all around. But the spirit of that Child has endured, bringing peace and good will, joy and hope — turning darkness into light.

I wish you a very merry Christmas — a Christmas merry with gifts given and received, a Christmas merry with Christmas trees and Christmas puddings, a Christmas merry and holy with the presence of children. But above all, I wish you a Christmas where in spirit and in truth you are in the presence of a child, the Christ Child, knowing within you a new birth of good will, joy, and peace.

A very merry Christmas to you,

Charles Martin

With Thy gracious favor, Almighty God, we beseech Thee to behold our universities, colleges, and schools so that knowledge may be increased among us and all good learning flourish and abound.

Bless all who teach and all who learn and grant that in humility of heart they may ever look unto Thee, who are the fountain of all wisdom; through Jesus Christ our Lord. Amen.

*Charles Martin**

---

*Prayer originally published in the St. Albans *Bulletin*, Autumn 1955.

VIII

Why St. Albans?

September 1955

Dear Friends,

Why St. Albans? Certainly there are the usual reasons: St. Albans builds character, prepares boys for college, develops leaders, makes informed churchmen — these are the kinds of reasons that embellish every school catalogue and slip easily from the lips of speechmakers. But in a deeper sense, why *are* we here? My own answer, simply put, is this: we are here primarily to maintain a family — a family that meets the basic needs of that curious human being called *boy*.

Every person needs to feel he belongs, that he is accepted by others. He must know that he is valued, both by a group and in that group's scheme of things. Such knowledge is necessary for self-respect and self-development.

At school a boy will do pretty much what every other boy does; on the other hand, he will also do that which he alone can do. He will find success in a way peculiar to himself and his abilities. I am sometimes surprised to witness the transformation a boy undergoes when he first tastes success, when he first wins a measure of recognition. I have seen a boy in scholastic difficulties changed into a respectable student by delivering a good speech before the student body, by painting a picture that won admiration, by being appointed to a responsible position.

Eric was such a boy. He was generally undistinguished at School. Both his brother and his parents were brilliant, and his father's mind overwhelmed me. Eric felt, no doubt, that members of his family did everything better than he. Hence, even though his Dad had the best of intentions, he had taken over Eric's personality. The boy just plodded along, doing as he was told, recognizing his own inadequacies and emptiness.

Then came an operetta. Eric, who was in the Glee Club, had a fairly good voice and was given a lead. He did a wonderful job, singing well and acting with an assurance and skill that were a joy to behold. I didn't know Eric had it in him; apparently no one else did, including his father. His father was transformed. He went around after the show congratulating everyone and being congratulated. His face beamed.

When Eric met his father after the performance, the man looked at his son with pride and humility. The father realized that his son had achieved something he himself could not; he was clearly awed. From that time on, Eric's life changed. It seemed like a miracle of conversion. He became a person who was respected in his own right. Eric was transformed into a new boy at home and at School, treated differently both by his family and his peers. A year later he graduated from St. Albans with a better record in his senior year than he had achieved in all his previous years of schooling. More important, he had gained self-respect. Today he is doing well at college, taking leads in plays, succeeding academically. Whether or not he will choose acting or music as a profession remains to be seen. In any case, I believe Eric has become a "real" person, one who will make a substantial contribution to life. Eric had been lost and was found, found through a success, found through using and developing a special gift.

Each boy needs to find such recognition. Indiscriminate praise that flows from general good will, devoid of discriminating perception, will never do it. Deep within him, a boy knows what he does and does not deserve. The School's duty is to know and nourish each lad's unique abilities. Such knowledge of boys, however, seldom comes readily. It may come easily and naturally; it may come about through the labor of a school career. Or unhappily (for such is the complexity of boys and such are the limitations of teachers), it may never come at all. In spite of these complexities and limitations, to help a boy know he is accepted and valued for himself is a primary responsibility of our School.

Even more important, a boy needs to know love. He has to feel he is cared for even when he is disagreeable and unpleasant. The environment in which an individual flourishes best is one of warm, understanding affection. However, love should not be equated with softness. Sometimes a boy learns only as he fails; true love does not always spare and protect. One of the finest teachers I have known is always exacting, demanding; however, he cares intensely for boys. While he may be rigorous and critical in the classroom, he also shows unending patience and concern. To these qualities boys respond in like manner; as a result, extraordinary learning takes place.

Along with love, boys need discipline. I don't mean the rod or demerits, although I have no objection to either if properly employed and understood. Boys need the security of knowing what they can and cannot do. They need certainties to govern their behavior. Authority that is just will always be accepted among boys: authority from one whom they feel trust and love is accepted most easily and helpfully. In boyhood as in life, discipline comes first from without and is imposed from above. Then, as the individual grows in security, it is internalized to become self-discipline. The School must meet this need both for security and discipline.

I have not yet mentioned studies. Surely the fundamental purpose of any school is to teach fundamentals. St. Albans bears a responsibility to hold boys to their highest capabilities, to enable them to take on the toughest that secondary school and college have to offer, and to graduate among the best. But a school can achieve its basic academic purpose only if every boy is considered as a whole and is developed as a balanced person in accordance with his own particular gifts.

It is good to remember that even though a boy has been well prepared academically for college, he may not always do well there. Boys sometimes do fail in college, but not because they are deficient in knowledge of academic subjects. Their failure may be due to any number of reasons — they cannot keep their noses to the grindstone, they spend too much time socializing, or they find the greener grass on the other side of the fence more tempting. A boy may fail in college — indeed in life — not because of the nature of his mental equipment but usually because his mind is unable to function to its fullest. Simply put, he has not become the self the good Lord intended him to be. Our job at St. Albans, then, is not only to train minds but also to nurture boys, of whom the mind is an essential part.

Finally, St. Albans is a Church school. Sometimes one of our masters chides me, "You speak of this as a Church school. If so, parents don't send their boys here for that reason. They send them here because we get boys into college and do a good job with them academically."

From one point of view, this statement is perfectly true. From another, it is nonsense. Some parents may choose St. Albans because of their deep commitment to the Church. However, I imagine the majority send their sons here because of the general attitude that attending a Church school is beneficial. Some may send their boys here for the prestige or because it is "the thing to do." In general, however, I would say that boys come to us because their families like our product. They know that our boys do well in college and in life. They like what our boys stand for and what they are. And that's sufficient reason for me.

What these parents like and desire for their sons is the product of a Christian education. Sacred Studies and chapel services do not make a Church school, although they are indispensable parts of it. A Church school is a fellowship in which human beings can grow and develop into the fullness of manhood that God purposed for them. It is a family in which the basic needs of individuals are met, in which a boy has the security to grow. That kind of family exists in its highest form only if it is part of the larger family, the Church, which in turn is made up of people who themselves are accepted, loved, and disciplined — not merely by others, but by God Himself.

I would like to think that you, the parents, and we, the schoolmasters, are raising a group of boys who will be a little wiser, somewhat more responsible, and even rather finer than our generation has been. That hope is not a simple one nor is it easily fulfilled. It is difficult for us to confer on our sons, our students, a wisdom and quality of character that we ourselves do not possess. To this end, we must all be open, receptive, even humble. If we are, then the Lord sometimes takes us and does with us even more than we desire or deserve. Perhaps if we are dedicated enough, He will — through us — bless those strangely worrisome and wonderful trusts, our boys. It is not enough that they grow in wisdom and stature. They must also grow in that quality of life that will create a better world than we have brought into existence.

To this end, let us remember St. Albans School in our prayers so that our institution may grow in favor with God and man. Let us dedicate ourselves anew to Him through whom all things are possible, even that finer world of which we dream.

Faithfully yours,

Charles Martin

O God, whose son underwent forty days of temptation,

Grant us, we beseech thee, the courage to resist indulgence and the strength to meet our responsibilities,

That thy purpose with us may be fulfilled;

Through Jesus Christ Our Lord. Amen.

Ferdinand Ruge

IX

Discipline

January 26, 1956

Dear Friends,

In this letter, I would like you to think with me in a general way about a basis of behavior: discipline. All of us—children, young people, adults—need discipline in our lives. We need it because discipline provides us with definition and certainty. Not only do we all need to know what the rules of the game are, but we also need to obey them. A new baby grows best in an environment where love is expressed through an ordered routine. Likewise, a boy in school responds most fully in a classroom in which exacting, definite discipline is maintained. The adult who has certainty and security in his life knows a measure of peace that others do not. When the home, the school, or the community is uncertain or loose in its standards, confusion and unhappiness are the normal results.

I have seen many lives made difficult and harmed by a lack of discipline or by uncertain discipline. However, I have seldom seen individuals harmed by overly severe discipline. The master who is soft as a person or weak in his requirements rarely blesses his students; on the contrary, he often hurts them. The home that is indulgent in attitude, uncertain in its standards, is the one in which bickering and battling are the order of the day.

Occasionally I find parents concerned lest by some punishment or severity they may twist or harm their child's personality. They fear a wound to the inner man that will show up in later life as a personality complex or internal disfigurement. Such an attitude is not unnatural when excessive attention to such matters is paid by psychologists, child guidance experts, and schoolmasters. Of course, we ought to be sensitive enough to avoid hurting others, particularly our children. More important than avoiding pain, however, is establishing a relationship of mutual respect and affection. Love—not the kind that is sentimental and soft, but real love with the iron of justice and right in it—is the basis of all good relationships. In a family in which respect and affection are found, mistakes can be made and forgiven, hurts can be given and healed, a firm hand can be vigorously applied and the punishment forgotten.

Discipline must be a fixed, unalterable part of the scheme of things. It has been my experience that a young person accepts without hesitation discipline that seems natural. He does not rebel against it, since to him it represents fairness. An incident that occurred some years ago remains fresh in my memory because I have seen it repeated over and over again. A boy came to board at School because he had been having difficulties at home. We had been reluctant to accept him, feeling that the home ought to face up to its problems and responsibilities rather than shift them to the School. But we did take the boy. He had been staying out late, going to bed when he chose, studying or not as he wished. Any discipline applied at home had resulted in a battle. There had been peace for no one, especially not for the boy.

After a few weeks with us, I commented to the boy on how much he seemed to be enjoying himself, in spite of our ordered living habits, which were certainly more exacting than those of his home. His response was, "Here I know what is expected of me, and there's no arguing about it because I know it just has to be."

I could understand. At school there is a routine that one has to accept. The routine at home had been unclear. The boy had been allowed to shape his actions according to his desires. To get his own way, all the boy had to do was to be unpleasant enough, and so he had been. Yet he wasn't really satisfied within himself. He needed and desired both a firm sense of direction and the sense of security that come from knowing what types of behavior were and were not permitted. We are all like that boy, whether or not we acknowledge it.

The attitude of discipline now common among us was discussed in a recent article that appeared in *The New York Times Magazine.* An American newsman portrayed the difference between discipline in an English home versus that in an American home. He drew no conclusions regarding which was superior; he merely sought to picture each accurately. In the English home, he noticed that parents took for granted that they were in control of the home situation, that they knew what was best for their children. He saw them as unwavering and certain in their requirements. The hour for bedtime was set; acceptable table manners were expected. A natural and definite order of behavior prevailed.

In contrast, the American home laid its emphasis on reason. The child was reasoned with as though he were an adult, and his cooperation was sought. Bedtime became a reasoned discussion on the necessity for sleep if one were to grow. At the table, consideration for others was explained but not always obtained. There may be some question as to which method develops the more mature individual. I am sure excellent arguments could be offered for both methods, but I do not believe anyone who has known the average English child as well as the average American child will doubt that the control of an English home produces a measure of order, tranquillity, and comfort frequently lacking in its American counterpart.

Some years ago, Walter Lippmann wrote a short article about education, the substance of which is as follows. He spoke of education as being a vertical rather than a horizontal process. A parent has something to give to his child; he cannot give it by trying to get down to the child's level or by being a buddy to him; no parent can fully enter into a child's world; he must always be and can only be a parent—not a buddy, not another child. Whether the parent recognizes it or not, he or she has something valuable to offer, among other things a set of standards, of values. These are given vertically, not horizontally. A child will accept discipline and standards from a parent who acts as a parent, but not from one whom he regards as another child.

Part of the problem of setting forth standards is the question of what other children do. It often seems as if we are the only parents who hold to high standards and make demands on our young people. Other people's children are allowed a measure of freedom that may seem to us like license. At least, such seems to be the case if we believe what our children tell us. And we do know that other children are allowed, or take, liberties we would not permit or would prefer not to permit our children to take.

Sometimes the problems of social behavior, of raising a child in a sophisticated community, bring such frustrations that parents seek to escape from them. While there are many good reasons for sending children off to boarding schools, doing so as an escape from the problems of living is not among them. The times in which we live are an indisputable fact. We and our children have to live in these times whether we like them or not. Children who are removed from today's problems will have to face them later in their lives. It has been my experience that often those who were withdrawn at early adolescence as a means of escaping from their environment and its problems often have a rough time when they have to face up to life's problems later on.

Perhaps the most perplexing dilemma with regard to discipline is ourselves. Certainties and standards with which we grew up as young persons no longer obtain; thus, our own principles vary; they are not always firmly rooted. This situation is both understandable and unfortunate. Indeed, rapid change is a characteristic of modern life. Without our own certainties of belief or of discipline, it is not easy for us to pass them on to our children. For those in this position—and the number includes many of us—there are no easy answers. We do live in a time of confusion and rapid change. It is difficult to know—much less to hold fast to—the abiding and to identify the transient, allowing it to pass by.

I commend to you the community that is the Church, an institution that has held fast to a set of standards and principles through the ages. More than that, the Church has within it a spirit, a quality of life, that enables us to accept and live by its standards. This institution has offered help to people in ages past and with no small measure of success.

This discussion may sound pedantic, stuffy, and unreasonable, and perhaps it is. I think not. American education and American life tend to be neither demanding nor exacting. Even American religious understanding tends to err on the side of softness. We see God in all His tenderness and compassion, His gentleness and love (which is good), but we neglect to see the strength in His will, the justice in His mercy, the iron in His law.

I write this letter before Lent. May I remind you that Lent is a wonderful season of the Church year that reminds us all that discipline is good and that God gives and expects much of us. Lent is a season during which I hope you will lay aside some of your usual busyness and give time to that which is really fundamental—relationships, not only your relationship with family, with your fellow men, but also with God." Lent is also a good time to remember that God never expects more of us than He will enable us to do.

To recapitulate briefly: your boy is an awfully nice one, an exceptionally fine one, but he is human. I believe it will help both you and him to live together in peace and in love if you are definite and certain in your requirements of him. He prospers and is secure as he knows what to expect. Expect much of him, but expect more of yourselves.

As parents we must always be prepared to be harder on ourselves than on anyone else, certainly harder than on our children. We should not expect miracles, however—either from ourselves or from our children. If with austerity and conviction we parents hold ourselves to high standards, then perhaps the grace of our Lord Jesus Christ may so work in and through us that our boys will come to know the self-discipline we would all have for them.

Faithfully yours,

Charles Martin

O God, who knowest the secret places of the heart,
Preserve us from self-deception.
Help us to see ourselves as we are and not as we think we are;
And through the fellowship of Thy Church
Enable us to find the courage and the strength to become more nearly what we would be. Amen.

Ferdinand Ruge

X

Change—Is It Possible?

April 10, 1956

Dear Friends,

This letter is addressed to parents who have reached or have gone beyond that delightful moment of maturity known as forty, parents who still have a problem or two in their lives or with their families. If you are not yet forty or if you have no such problems, read no further!

"But you can't do much to change yourself when you're forty, can you?" That question was posed in a half-worried, half-amused manner by friends of mine, parents of a twelve-year-old boy. We had been discussing their son, who was, they believed, not developing as they felt he should. Although their son was a normal, healthy boy, his parents (like so many of us with a high sense of responsibility) were worriers, fussing too much, expecting too much. What the boy needed was some good healthy neglect. Even though I made this point rather vigorously, and they accepted my advice, doubts lingered.

What, indeed, can you do to change yourself, whether you are twenty, forty, or sixty? If you are a chronic worrier, it is fine to realize that you shouldn't worry, but it is something else again to actually stop doing so. When your son is not home by an appointed hour, you worry, unable to control your vivid imagination. If you are by temperament one whose anger is close to the surface and you do not possess the virtue of patience, you find it extremely difficult to refrain from commenting on your daughter's room that is knee-deep in disorder.

While we may try to be patient, long-suffering, understanding, and loving, these desires may frequently evaporate under the stress of hearing children squabble, listening to the noise of the phonograph rending the quiet of the neighborhood, or being jarred by the telephone's constant ringing.

Most of us have a pretty good idea of the qualities we would like to or think we ought to possess. Living up to those expectations, however, is quite another matter. Then, too, problems arise when we try to fashion a spouse, child, or other individual into what we think he or she should be—at least, so I have noticed.

Whatever your age, you may feel that there is not much you can do to change your basic personality traits. Furthermore, you can do even less about changing those of the other fellow. While I do not believe that change is ever altogether impossible, I do know this: before any change can take place, we have to learn to know and accept ourselves and other people as they are.

Whenever I talk to a young couple who are about to be married, I always say to them, "John, you can't coerce Mary into becoming a different person, the kind of person you think she ought to be, or the ideal you had always imagined she would be. And Mary, you can't nag John into being the kind of husband you hoped he would be. Human beings can't change other human beings. Husbands can't change wives; neither can wives change husbands."

Likewise, all the anxiety and driving demands you place upon your boy will not hurry his growth and development one whit. You may cause your son to be nervous and unhappy, but he won't be greatly altered in moving toward the direction you wish. No matter how others may fuss and fume, a boy has to be himself. We would all do well to see ourselves as we are and learn to live with that self not complacently, but in peace.

I don't mean to suggest that we ought to accept our world and all that is in it exactly as it is. We have to strive, to uphold ideals, to seek answers. Mere acceptance of the status quo would signify stagnation, even death. Those who are impatient or ill-tempered can, with time and effort, learn to be more patient or less prone to anger. Behavior may be changed within certain limits. Still, when all is acknowledged, we are still left with the need to learn to accept ourselves—with all our strengths and our shortcomings. Ultimately, we have to love ourselves—and that is not always easy.

Whence cometh the courage to change? Where does one acquire the serenity that, with deep inner quiet, permits him to live with a peace that passeth understanding? How does one discover the wisdom that enables him to choose among a multitude of possibilities, none of which seems black or white? There may be simple answers to these questions. If there are, I am suspicious of them.

One does not acquire courage, serenity, wisdom, or any other virtue. One receives these qualities as gifts. Thus a parent cannot change himself or his child. Sometimes, though, if the parent is patient, understanding, wise, kind, and loving, these qualities working in and through him may bring change. These qualities are of God Himself. God alone can make us, change us, reorder our lives. Not from ourselves but from beyond and outside ourselves do we receive all that we have, all that we are, all that we would be.

If we would undertake the seemingly impossible task of changing the direction of our growth or aiding someone else in his or her growth, the best course of action I know is for us to associate ourselves with others who are seeking to do the same thing. Strength is found in seeking common values; more important, strength is found in the common spirit that enables us to hold fast to those values. Admitting to a bias, I have observed that the Church comes nearest to being the ideal group that can provide the strength we need to change and to live as we would like to. Those who have eyes to see and ears to hear find in the Church a spirit of understanding and wisdom, of patience and sympathy, that enables them to attain and hold fast to these ideals. The Church offers a quality of life that can change even the toughest among us. It offers a means of growing for the better, of changing that curious animal who is you or me.

St. Albans is part of the Church. When boys come to us, they enter a life in which they are expected to work and play hard, to consider one another, and to work for the common good. Something happens to the boys. Parents say, "I've never seen him work so hard." "He's a different boy around the house." What happens is that the boys have entered a community that possesses a set of standards, of ideals. The quality of life in the School enables boys to change and to grow.

To return to the question posed by my friends—there are no easy answers to changing ourselves at forty or anyone else at any age. And we should realize that fact when we grow impatient with our boy who is not living up to expectations, or when we are unhappy about ourselves because we are not as we would like to be. But it is heartening to know that if we are serious enough in our quest, some change can be and is brought about in even the most difficult of us through the fellowship of the Church, one of whose purposes is to redeem and to make new.

Faithfully yours,

Charles Martin

With students and Cleopatra III in the St. Albans Common Room, 1957.

O Lord our Christ, may I have Thy mind and Thy Spirit.
Make me an instrument of thy peace:
where there is hatred, let me sow love;
where there is injury, pardon;
where there is discord, union;
where there is doubt, faith;
where there is despair, hope;
where there is darkness, light;
where there is sadness, joy;
for Thy mercy and for Thy truth's sake.

St. Francis of Assisi

XI

Love That Suffereth Long

November 8, 1956

Dear Friends,

This letter is about love. While love may seem an unusual subject for a parent letter, I believe it is not. I meet love in parents, in boys, and in masters. I encounter love in ordinary relationships and in the midst of extraordinary events. Love always blesses. Occasionally, an unusual expression of love brings new insights about life itself. But let me tell you of love, or of one of its aspects, in terms of the common experiences of school life.

A father visited me, relating a moving tale of a lad I had once known. The boy graduated from a good school—more through the efforts of the school and his parents than through his own efforts—and went off to college. There, however, lacking support from school and home, he lasted only a few months. For a while he did nothing but enjoy life on his own terms. Then he got a job, but it turned out that he and work didn't get along well. Moving from job to job, from failure to failure, the boy was always enthusiastic about prospects to come and always unaware of the failures of the past. Worse, he remained unmindful of the reasons for failure that so plainly existed within himself. Every time the boy failed, his parents picked him up. Bad debts were met, hurts were healed, new opportunities were found. Finally the boy entered the army. In its discipline and routine the lad now appears to be finding himself.

It was a good experience to listen to the father and to meet his love. He felt he had no more than the usual share of problems. He had tried to deal with situations as they arose and to act as any parent would, but he had a quality of patience, a forgiving love that most of us do not possess. His love for his son glowed, and every word carried a moving conviction because of it. I felt warmed by his love and better for it.

Still, I was deeply troubled. The boy, in my judgment, had been helped too much, spared too much. He had never been allowed to experience the full consequences of his actions. When difficulties arose, he always looked to his father for help, and his father always came to his rescue because he could not stand the pain of seeing his son suffer. And he said, in a somewhat embarrassed manner, "Perhaps I shouldn't have helped so much, but you can't see a boy hurt without doing something about it."

The father's love, fine as it is, seemed not deep or strong enough to bear the suffering of watching his boy endure pain without the father interfering, even though to stand aside was to help the boy most, ultimately to show kindness. Even now, when the boy seemed to be discovering his true self in the army, the father, apprehensive about hurts, was trying to assure his son a better future than he was likely to have in the military. My help was being sought to get the lad back into college.

I expressed my admiration and appreciation for the support given the boy and then gently tried to say what I knew my friend did not want to hear—that I felt the boy should remain in the army. I suggested that he be allowed to make his own decisions, stand on his own two feet, accept the consequences of his own actions, work out his own salvation. Although the father agreed verbally, he differed inwardly. He left thinking that I was unsympathetic, that I had failed him.

I have been disturbed by our conversation. Naturally, one

does not like to cause pain. Although it is much more pleasant to say the expected and the agreeable, in conscience I could not. The father's love, deep and rich though it was, had failed to allow the boy to profit from his own failures. Like so many of us, he could not let his son plumb the depths and then fight his own way up. Regardless of hurt to ourselves, there are times when love demands that we stand aside, watch those whom we love, and do nothing except what is necessary—suffer long and be kind.

I saw another parent recently—a widow with one child. Hers is a fine lad, but a self-willed and obstinate one. His first months at college were unhappy, and he wanted to leave. Sympathetically but firmly his mother urged him to stay. Midyear examinations came, and he was still uneasy. Reluctantly she gave her consent for her son to leave college—a difficult decision. She had planned during a lifetime for college for him.

In the navy the boy encountered difficult moments. The world of the navy was vastly different from that of home and school. Orders had to be obeyed, all sorts and conditions of men had to be lived with. His mother counseled, helped where she could, worried about whether she had made the right decision, even though she knew that the decision had already been made and that the consequences had to be endured. The boy had to work his own way out. He suffered as he fell, but his mother suffered more. It would have been easier and less painful for her to have borne his hurts than to watch him suffer them himself. The lessons he will learn remain to be seen, but his mother still waits, her deep love permitting the boy to work out his own salvation—even if the experience must involve suffering.

I used to fear for another boy's physical safety. Peter tantalized others, making himself a perpetual nuisance. Even though his classmates disliked him, he seemed to have no understanding of how much he irritated them. Actually, I think his actions were a perverse way of securing their attention, even their affection. There was no end of trouble between him and the other boys, but his parents' love was deep, wise, and strong—so great that they were able to let him learn from his own mistakes.

I remember the beginning of his regeneration. In the Common Room a little boy, inoffensive and quiet but goaded beyond endurance, let go a punch at Peter that moved his nose to the side of his face. The nose required two operations. Peter's parents were wonderful, offering understanding and helpfulness. Peter became subdued for a while. I believe that because of his public humiliation, Peter began to gain better insight into himself. However, he was basically still Peter.

He stayed in college only a brief time. Then came the army and a short stint of work. Although some pain was always involved, at the same time there was growth. And that growth came through the love of his parents who sympathized, who supported. Most of all, these parents allowed experience to teach its lessons. Peter returned to college. He will graduate and become a useful citizen, more useful than most, because he is more sensitive than most. He will encounter more pain, but he will be able to endure it and be finer for it.

From among these experiences, one truth is clear: each boy has the right to be a person, the right to make his own mistakes, even the right to suffer. It is difficult to give the love that allows such independence. This is true from the first time a boy crosses a busy street on his own to the time when he first drives a car. It is true when he leaves home to go to college or when, as a young adult, he makes a decision that conflicts with that of his elders. It is natural as a parent to seek to protect the child. However, it is natural and right, too, to allow the young person to learn through the results of his own actions, even though it may cause anguish to himself and others. This is indeed asking much of us as parents and schoolmasters, for it requires a deep, strong love, a love with more iron in it than the self-protective love most of us know for our children. From those to whom much is given—and children are no small blessing—much is expected.

A teacher of some insight once said, "Love knows no limit to its endurance, no end to its trust, no fading of its hope: it can outlast anything. It is, in fact, the one thing that still stands when all else has fallen."

Faithfully yours,

Charles Martin

O Lord, our Heavenly Father
Who has committed to us the care of boys,
Bless us with wise and understanding hearts that we may demand neither too much nor too little of them.
And grant us such a measure of love that we may nurture our boys to the fullness of manhood that Thou has purposed for them.
Through Him who was a Teacher, Jesus Christ our Lord. Amen.

Charles Martin

XII

You Don't Understand

March 22, 1957

Dear Friends,

"You don't understand!" "That might have been true in your day, but times have changed!" "We don't do it that way anymore!" "It's no use. You wouldn't understand." These comments probably sound quite familiar to you.

How *do* you understand? How *do* you come close to your boy? How *do* you establish an easy relationship with your children that has as its hallmarks warmth, companionship, and shared confidences? I'm not sure I know, but I've thought about the matter considerably. No doubt you have also. Further thought about the matter may help, for we all desire a close relationship with our children.

Recently I heard a parent say, "I didn't know my son until he went to college." I understood what she meant. The boy had learned much away from home and had grown in maturity. The parent had developed a new perspective, and both had been freed of some of the tensions of close living. They saw each other in a new light; thus, there was a meeting of the minds and of persons. More often I have heard parents say, "I want to enjoy my son, for in a few years he will be off to college and then he'll be lost. It's college, military service, marriage, and he's gone." I can understand that feeling, too.

Why some fathers and sons are close and others are not is never easy to fathom. As I think through my experiences, it is difficult to make generalizations on the subject. There is, of course, an occasional natural congeniality that blesses. Some parents and children are close because they are made that way. They share the same interests, likes, and dislikes. "He's his father's son, all right." "How like his mother he is." When that is the case, those fortunate ones can be grateful to the good Lord and go about deepening their relationship. However, I do not believe that such congeniality occurs naturally; it develops. Normally, even with those most dear to us, differences exist. Interests, personalities, and worlds separate us. It is not easy for an individual to enter into someone else's world, particularly that of another generation.

I was invited to dinner one night at the home of a friend. While we were having coffee, my friend's son asked to be excused to do his homework. He was excused, but not without a lecture on study habits. Bill was polite to his father but restive, easing away before his Dad had finished. It was evident to me that this was not the first lecture he had heard on the subject.

I was amazed not at the lecture but at my friend's lack of understanding. An able, successful lawyer, he loved the abstract. With his keen, incisive mind he could cut the abstract to pieces, lay it bare, and then make it clear. The boy shied away from the abstract but was good with practical matters; he was also wonderful with people. He and his father were very different, but the father did not recognize it. One could see that the father not only expected his son to think as he did, but also to be as he was.

My friend's wife relieved the tension as Bill left the table with, "John is so able that he takes for granted that Bill will be like him instead of realizing he has some of his mother's traits." I could understand why Bill was closer to his mother.

Boys can be guided and nurtured. They can even slowly, very slowly, be changed. They cannot be remade, nor can they be put into molds for which they were not created. One cannot make an engineer out of a boy just because that career presents a good opportunity in the business world. One cannot make a quiet, reserved lad into an outgoing extrovert, happy in all his social relationships. A boy's nature and interests are determined by his genes, by what his Creator meant him to be. He wants to be accepted and loved for himself. Any boy (as any one of us) desperately needs the sympathy and love that will nurture and guide him from what he is into what he ought to be. A lad must, even as a child, be a person in his own right, always moving toward complete independence. He must be respected and loved for his unique qualities, whatever his stage of development.

Still, I do not mean to imply that there cannot be discipline in relations between parents and children. There must be. Every boy needs to know what he can and cannot do. Certainties give order and stability to life; they help a boy grow as he should. It is a weak, soft perversion of love that accepts less than a boy's best. Of course, unwise, unfair discipline can and does separate. However, discipline in love makes for respect and closeness.

Boys and parents meet in many ways. I sat next to a father at a wrestling match in which his son was wrestling. Father and son shared a close communion, a common interest not only in wrestling but also in all forms of athletics. They could discuss and appreciate an intricate leg-hold in wrestling or the beautiful grace of a baseball bat perfectly meeting a ball for a hit. A love of athletics, or any shared interest—be it music, people, the outdoors, or art—brings boys and parents together. The deeper the interest, the more it demands of a person, the higher and more meaningful it is in life, the closer it brings individuals.

Boys and parents come together not only through shared interests but also through all forms of shared living. A friend told me, "I went to a good school and am very grateful for it, but my education really began in the Fifth Form when my Dad took sick and became an invalid. Mother and I went through some rough times together, and I grew up in a few weeks. Mother and I came to appreciate each other more." Through shared experiences, we move closer to one another. Whether we share trouble, sorrow, fun, happiness, or just daily routines, these experiences unite us.

I believe that we come closest together through shared love. Those who have common ideals and values, who love the same person, will inevitably draw near to one another. Our lives are most deeply united as we give ourselves in love, as we sacrifice for or live for another individual.

A boy and his parents can meet most deeply through worship. Religion can deeply unite or, alas, can deeply separate, because it deals with the worship of ultimate values and the ultimate Person. Often we fail to recognize the power of worship to unite, for like most things that are natural and fundamental we are either unaware of them or else take them for granted.

A boy at St. Albans is having a rough time at home; neither he nor his parents know why things are so difficult. At the root of the problem, I believe, is a deep conflict within the boy between the values his family professes to worship and those they actually follow. While they profess to worship God, in reality they worship the gods of the world and its common values. The boy tells me proudly how his father "fixes" things in traffic court, how great is his father's influence. I hear of important friends, of new Cadillacs, and of a sumptuous social life. The boy tells me these things because he is ashamed. He cannot admit that fact to himself, so he talks boldly and proudly to cover up his shame. At home he does not have to disguise his real feelings; bitter recriminations, resentments, and harsh separation are the results. While he may not be aware of it, the boy holds one set of values, his parents another. A belief in antithetical value systems results in violent separation.

Ironically, the more one tries to become close to another person, the more one may fail. Closeness happens as a result of something else. We can try to understand our son, to respect and love him as I have suggested, but we cannot worry ourselves into a good relationship with him and, in a sense, we cannot work ourselves into a good one. Such a relationship just happens. It seems to happen most often and most fully when we give ourselves to someone beyond ourselves and particularly to Him who is patient, wise, understanding, gentle, and loving. Through Him we see our boy as he is and as he ought to be. In Him we can find the spirit that enables us to know companionship and love.

We all desire to be close to our children, to love them, and to have them love us. As we see and love them for what they are, we most often realize our desires. Closeness comes about through shared common interests and through love, ideally the love of God.

So stated, it sounds simple. For most of us, though, understanding takes some unusual living and not a little help from One who has done a large measure of working and fussing over His children—God, the Father of us all.

Faithfully yours,

Charles Martin

The St. Albans School Prayer

Vouchsafe Thy blessing, we beseech Thee, O Lord, upon this School and upon all other works undertaken in Thy fear and for Thy glory; and grant that all who serve Thee here, whether as teachers or learners, may set Thy holy will ever before them, and seek always to do such things as are pleasing in Thy sight, that so both the Church and the Commonwealth of this land may benefit by their labors, and they themselves may attain unto everlasting life; through Jesus Christ our Lord. Amen.

Adapted by Bishop Satterlee *

*Henry Yates Satterlee, first Bishop of Washington, D.C., served from 1896-1908.

XIII

Public vs. Independent Schools

September 10, 1957

Dear Friends,

I am taking advantage of the quiet of the Labor Day holiday to write this letter. But I am taking no chances about insuring quiet! I have put my car out of sight behind the building, locked the School's front door, and closed the hall door and my study door. School, however, is always a busy place, so I don't really expect to remain undisturbed. Summer or winter, Sundays or weekdays, vacations or terms, something of interest is always happening here.

I have just finished writing to the chaplains of the colleges which our June graduates will attend. For me, this act marks the beginning of each new school year. Although I always dislike seeing a class leave, I feel better after writing to the chaplains and commending our boys to their care. I know, then, that someone on the new campus will be interested in our boys—someone who will assist them as needed and get in touch with me when I can help. I want our boys to know that even though they have graduated from St. Albans, they will remain part of the School family—that we are concerned for them not only while they are in college or in military service but also later in life.

Now for the new year! In recent weeks I have been thinking much about a statement a student's mother made to me: "I'm so glad John is at St. Albans! I had to do a lot of convincing to get my husband to agree to send him here. He felt strongly that every boy ought to go to public school." I talked with the mother at some length about the questions her husband had raised, and I should like to discuss them with you.

At the outset, let me give you some of my background in education. I attended public school and, for a time, so did three of my children. I served as an elected member of a public school board for several years; over the years I have been closely associated with those active in public education. On the other hand, I have also been associated with church schools for most of my life. All four of my children have attended church schools. At present I am headmaster of what I believe to be a fine one. Therefore, I feel I have some appreciation for both independent and public education. At the same time, I am at St. Albans because I believe the kind of education offered here is worth giving my life to.

Public and independent education both make valuable contributions to our American culture. Each serves a special purpose. Church schools have been in existence longer. The Episcopal Academy in Philadelphia, where I served as teacher and chaplain before I came to St. Albans, has been in existence longer than the Constitution of the United States. Trinity School in New York was founded not long after Peter Stuyvesant was stomping about New Amsterdam on his peg leg.

While public schools have not been in existence as long as private schools, they are certainly doing a larger business. The overwhelming majority of our young people attend them. What the future will bring to public and independent schools no one can fathom, except that each will continue in its present capacity only as it serves the community well.

One often hears, "I went to public school and received a good education. So can my son. He doesn't need to attend private school." While that observation is natural, it is hardly valid. A boy can receive a good education in public school, but not because his father did. Individuals differ; schools differ; the times certainly differ. A boy ought to attend a school where he can best develop his potential. For some boys, that choice will be a public school. For others, depending upon the boy and the quality of the public schools, the choice will be an independent school.

This much is certain: a boy today needs a very fine secondary school education if he is to be admitted to the college he chooses *and* if he is to remain there. Even more important, life today with all its confusion and change demands the best education possible for every boy.

Twelve years of schooling may be ordained by law for all, but a good education is not necessarily a byproduct. A "good" education—whether in public or independent school—derives from planning, wise decisions, hard work, and from the ability to adapt to changing times.

Another familiar comment I hear: "A boy has to live in the world with all sorts of people, and he may as well start living with them right now in public school." This is an understandable attitude. A boy does, indeed, have to live in the world with all sorts, and he may have to go into the military and live with all manner of men. Certainly he ought to be prepared to know all kinds of people, but there is not just one type of school that can best prepare him. Normally a school like St. Albans offers a better chance to meet this need than do many high schools, for it draws its student body from a wide area of American life and also has a substantial representation of boys from other nations. Of necessity, a public high school reflects the immediate community and is likely to be relatively homogeneous. The student body of a public school in one urban or suburban community will be quite different from that in another. Rarely does a public school in a large community have a varied student body, while any private school worth its salt will have, or will be striving to have, students who represent a wide range of social and economic backgrounds.

When that is understood, I think it must still be realized that it is important for boys as they develop to get out in society as much as possible, to meet it as it is—in its rawness and its fineness.

Thus, I urge our boys in the upper forms to get jobs during the summer, to meet people, and to enjoy new experiences. Education can never be adequate if it is confined to formal schooling alone.

The experience of meeting and living with people different from ourselves, however, does not necessarily result in understanding. Some Americans, for example, go abroad and see little. Living among people less fortunate than ourselves does not inevitably develop sympathy or empathy. Conversely, living among the poor and suffering can sometimes cause us to become bitter. On the other hand, dwelling among the rich and famous may make us covetous, or it may make us contemptuous of the clay feet that all human beings have—even the great.

No, meeting all sorts and conditions of men in school or in life is not the key to human understanding and sympathy. Such qualities can be found in the sensitivity to and concern for others that come from having Christian ideals. What we worship determines what we shall be. If we worship a God who is compassionate, merciful, understanding, just, and loving, these qualities will show forth in our lives.

A school like St. Albans exists to teach reading, writing, and arithmetic, and to teach these subjects well. But more important, St. Albans exists to enable every boy to know and worship God. If he knows and worships God, he will have a set of values that will enable him to live richly with all kinds of men—to live with sensitivity, purpose, and a sense of justice.

Independent schools are sometimes accused of being snobbish. I am sure such a charge may at times be justified, for the sin of snobbishness exists everywhere. But I don't for a moment believe that snobbishness is a peculiar property of independent schools. Sin is found wherever there are human beings.

The sin of snobbishness takes many forms. The intellectual kind looks down its nose at ignorance and at philistinism. The opposite type, often found among young people, looks at anyone who respects intellectual achievement as a "square" or a "brain." Among adults, this kind of snobbery looks at poverty as a sign of degradation; still another sees wealth as a sign of dishonesty. Yet another variety considers having the "right" family tree as being essential for entry into the Kingdom of Heaven. Unless a person is very careful, careful to the extent of getting help from One outside himself, he may see snobbishness only in the other fellow or in the other fellow's school. It is always easy to see the mote in another person's eye and miss the beam in one's own. No school, no group, no individual is free from such faults.

God forbid that any of us should be plagued by snobbishness! And, of course, it is God who will forbid it—if we are wise enough to see that flaw in ourselves. As we worship Him we shall be kept sensitive to all sorts and conditions of human beings, sensitive to pride and snobbery everywhere, even to the devastating pride and snobbishness that exist within ourselves—often unknown and unacknowledged.

The problems of education today are many, yet the opportunities are great. I doubt that any public school or any independent school can meet all these problems or take advantage of all these opportunities. I discuss such matters with my colleagues. I work at them myself. I pray about them. Sometimes I see answers and give thanks. Often I see no answers, but I give thanks anyway, for one thing I have, and that is confidence in the Teacher. We may not always know the way. We may not always do the kind of job we ought to do, but we always know that as we give ourselves freely to Him and as we recognize our limitations and are deeply concerned about them, He will use us, and use us for good. Perhaps He may even use us enough to justify the act of trust that you have made by placing your sons here with us.

Faithfully yours,

Charles Martin

O God, who hast commanded that no man should be idle: Give us grace to employ all our talents and faculties in the service appointed to us, that whatsoever our hand findeth to do, we may do it with our whole might. Amen.

*James Martineau**

**A Boy's Prayer Book*, p. 48.

XIV

Hard Work

September 29, 1958

Dear Friends,

I write this letter to you about our responsibility to that becoming, ever-changing, ever-new person—your boy. When questioned about what he did at school on a certain day, he may reply "Nothing." Or to "Anything new today?" with "Nope." Or to "How's the new master?" with "All right." Although this creature may at times seem strangely uncommunicative, he is well worth cultivating. If your boy is not pressed too much, if he is met at his own level, if his interests are respected, and if he feels his privacy is not being invaded, he may frequently reveal a wealth of news and intelligent ideas. More important, he may reveal that he is becoming and, occasionally, that he has already become, a new person. That is the best news a parent can have.

At the beginning of the school year, when we are all fresh and eager to begin, full of hopes and aspirations, we are all more receptive to the new and better able to grow. There is a lot of growing, both mental and physical, that I would like to see in our School, not only among boys, but also among parents and masters.

Right now I am chiefly concerned with growth that centers

on a value for which I have inordinate respect—work. I would like to see all of us increase our capacity for long, sustained, hard work. St. Albans has always valued work. I did not bring the idea here, nor did I develop it. It was here already. Dr. Lucas loved work and communicated that love. He held himself and others to rigorous standards of excellence. From what I can learn, his predecessor, Mr. Church, did the same. Of that heritage I am proud.

Yesterday I drove down to the football field because I was in a hurry—or thought I was. A number of boys were watching the late practice. All of them had driven down, too, perhaps because they were in a hurry but more probably because their cars had been at hand. And who would think of walking while a car was at hand! Perhaps too many automobiles, too many escalators, too many push buttons are at hand. The whole direction of American life is toward easier, more comfortable—but not necessarily better—living.

I was amused, but also troubled by two incidents that occurred recently. A ten-year-old boy was asked to raise my car window. He wrestled with the stiff handle and then complained, "Why don't you have those buttons that raise the window?" A few days later, a husky lad was watching a Western on the television set. To my request to switch the channel, he responded, "Gee, why don't we have one of those remote-control gadgets to save getting up and down from your chair so often?"

Life today is physically hard for only a few. We don't work today as former generations did. We can at once be grateful for this and recognize that something valuable has been, or can be, lost—toughness, hardness, endurance, the ability to "take it." It is good for us to make life easier and more comfortable—within limits. I am inclined to feel that the limits in many directions have been far exceeded. We used to walk, to climb, to carry, to struggle. If we are to be strong physically, we need the difficult and the demanding, just as we need it if we are to be at our best in any area of our lives.

Schools have been asked to do a great many things they ought not to do, and they have assumed responsibilities for many things they ought not have. We at St. Albans need to set our sights straight and not go off on tangents. St. Albans exists to give rough, exacting academic discipline in relation to One who sets standards for each of us. But we are all of one piece. We cannot do the best job academically without doing the best job physically.

I believe that every boy is better for some exercise that is vigorous enough to make bed welcome and sleep come easily. I like to see the glow of health and the vitality of body that come from being outdoors, roughing it a bit. Of course, I do realize that not every boy will love the outdoors or become an athlete. The Lord hasn't created all boys in the same mold.

While I don't expect all of our boys to play football, I do want them to have the opportunity. I believe that football gives a kind of elemental physical exercise that boys are better for having experienced. More important than having every boy play football, I want all to have some good stiff exercise. To that end, we are including a session of calisthenics for everyone in both the Lower and Upper Schools. In addition, for the Upper School we have constructed an obstacle course to be used by those not taking football. This obstacle course won't make a Marine out of a boy, but I believe it will make for better arms and shoulders, better legs and lungs.

A new boy came to our School last fall. He worked harder than he had ever worked before in his life, but when the marking period ended, he found this comment on his report: "Ward is coming along. He is working hard according to his lights, but his lights are not yet bright enough. He needs to learn a new standard of work, since he is capable of doing much better."

Ward and his parents were taken aback, but Ward accepted the criticism with courage. He learned to use his time more effectively. He stretched mentally, learned new capacities, and worked as he had never dreamed he could. By the end of the year he knew a joy and a satisfaction beyond anything he had ever experienced. Something like this I should like to see not only for our boys but also for the rest of us. I should like our lights of work to burn more brightly.

This brightness will not come merely because we demand it of our boys. We must first demand it of ourselves. I think of a master I once knew who was always demanding, sometimes even hard and rough. Parents were occasionally troubled because they thought he was too exacting. But boys were rarely troubled. They saw that however demanding the master was of them, he was more demanding of himself. No matter how hard they worked, he worked harder. No matter how much concentration, patience, or effort he demanded of them, he demanded more of himself. More important, he cared; they knew and appreciated this fact.

That master presents a lesson. The good intentions and aspirations we have for our children become realities only as we demand more of ourselves than we do of them or of any other person. We can never with success shift our responsibilities or our work. Occasionally a troubled parent entrusts his boy to us with an almost audible sigh of relief. This parent feels that in a school like St. Albans, his or her son will be successful. Although I am always flattered by such confidence, I know we do not always deserve it. If any boy is to grow into his best self, it will not be through the School alone, no matter how hard we may work. We and that boy will need all the understanding, patience, and love the parent and home can give. Such requires a good measure of that virtue called hard work.

I am not unmindful of the School's responsibility. Paradoxically, I know that we have as much trouble with boys who work too hard as with boys who do not work hard enough. When I hear from a master that a boy won't work, I am troubled. Sometimes neither the home nor the school can motivate a boy to give his best, no matter how hard we try, for none of us is all-wise; indeed, there are quite a few people on earth whom even the Almighty One seems unable to help. But we shall get a lot further with boys and with ourselves when, like the master I mentioned, we demand of ourselves hard, painstaking, long-suffering, and loving work.

One kind of work to which we need to dedicate ourselves is that of so understanding and loving our boys that we allow them to grow without too much interference. To arrive at maturity, boys must learn to fight their own battles, make their own decisions, and suffer from their own mistakes. We need to love our boys with an active, sustaining love that makes for confidence, strength, and independence—not with the protective, possessive love that makes for weakness and may tragically defeat its own ends. To so love our children is no small task, even for the wisest of parents. Yet there is no joy greater than to know the satisfaction that results from seeing a boy develop his strengths and use his abilities to the fullest.

How does one go about developing this capacity for hard work? I don't know the answer, and I would distrust anyone who thought he did. One cannot learn to become a parent, teacher, or person in ten easy lessons. One grows into his best self as he works at it under Him and in the spirit of Him who is the chief Worker, the Creator of heaven and earth and all that is in them.

I can make one suggestion, however, using the following illustration. A new boy arrives at St. Albans. He is unaccustomed to working hard; his standards differ from those he finds here. But he likes what he finds, and he seeks to live by the values around him. Although this requires strenuous effort on his part, his task is made easier because everyone else is working in the same manner toward similar goals. The spirit of the School, one that endorses sustained effort, works through and in the boy. As we parents and teachers become members of this group, whose values are high and whose spirit enables us to achieve these values, then we become more nearly the persons God intended us to be. When we know strength and self-fulfillment in ourselves, we will be better equipped to help and understand that extraordinarily malleable yet extraordinarily tough creature committed to us called boy.

Faithfully yours,

Charles Martin

O God, who hast revealed Thyself in the glory of the heavens and in the burning bush, in the still small voice, and in the dread power of the hydrogen bomb; make us aware of Thy presence as Thou comest in judgment through the events of our time.

Grant us to stand in awe and to sin not. Enable us to use the fearful powers Thou hast permitted us to know that we may work not toward man's destruction, but toward his fulfillment.

Lift us above the suspicions and fears of our day that we may bring righteous and just peace among all men. And this we ask, anxious, yet quiet in Thee; perplexed, yet certain in Thee; weak, yet strong in Thee, through Him who is the savior of us all, Jesus Christ our Lord. Amen.

Charles Martin

XV

Education in Our Times

November 1958

Dear Friends,

It has been more than a year now since the Russians announced their successful launching of a satellite. Spaceships are no longer a matter of fiction but of sober science. Planets are, or will soon be, our neighbors. While such an achievement is glorious, it is not an entirely happy one for Americans. The Russian success marked another in a series of shattering defeats our nation has met with in recent years.

The launching of Sputnik had been preceded by the successful flight of an intercontinental ballistic missile, "the ultimate weapon." Americans who naively saw Uncle Sam as being capable of licking whomever he chose, as being bigger and better than any other nation, were shocked—as were not a few of the uncommitted nations of the world. The United States, rich and powerful beyond all others, able to produce both prosperity and hydrogen bombs, had fallen behind another world power. We lost prestige and power.

Nor had the home situation been gratifying. Newspapers had been full of pictures of rioting mobs, of brutal, bloody faces, of children going to school at bayonet point. Such scenes came not from Moscow, but from Little Rock, Arkansas. America—land of the free, home of brotherhood and good will—was made painfully aware of the inequality between races. The Western world was dismayed, but nations beyond the Iron Curtain rejoiced. We lost prestige and power.

Yet the impact of these events at home and abroad may be viewed not with pessimism but with hope. Perhaps these events may signify our salvation. As a nation, we have in the past seemed to be very sure of ourselves, even arrogant, in our assumption of technical superiority and moral righteousness. It is good for us to learn that we cannot always be first, that we cannot always be right. It is good to suffer what we can hope will be a great blow to our pride. More important, it is good for us to be humbled, for only then can we learn to grow.

It may be that God in His infinite and inscrutable wisdom has allowed these humbling experiences to come upon us that we, no longer blinded by pride, may learn more fully the secrets of His universe and become spiritually more aware and more useful to Him.

Although these occurrences may appear to be unrelated to our life at St. Albans, I believe they are relevant not only to our School's future, but also to the future of education. You and I are dedicated to nurturing boys in a way that will prepare them to take part courageously, but humbly—and, we hope, nobly—in a world that is rapidly expanding into the mysterious and awesome grandeur of God's spacious firmament on high.

In part because of recent Russian advances, I have frequently been asked by alumni and parents during the past year, "What are you doing in science and mathematics at St. Albans?" It is, of course, a natural question in these days of satellites, missiles, and grim comparisons with Russia. Like anyone touched at the quick of his interest, I respond immediately and fully. I tell of our new Lower School science courses, of our advanced chemistry and physics for college credit in the Upper School. I launch into a description of our math courses, with algebra taught a year earlier than in most schools. And I tell of the "new math" that has actually been with us for years and of advanced math taught at college level for college credit.

I always finish answering such questions by emphasizing other subjects, for I want to make it clear that we are not trying to develop scientists at St. Albans. We are trying to develop boys who may become scientists if they so choose or anything else they choose—boys whose capacities will be expanded, whose ideals will be high, who will have grown into their own pattern of manhood.

It is incumbent upon us in these times to remember that a boy learns Russian, French, mathematics, and history because in and out of class someone gives him confidence when he is shy and diffident, courage when he falters, and discipline when he needs it. This is good education, in which each of us has a share. The School has been given the opportunity of seeing that more math, science, language, and history are taught and taught well. We have been given the opportunity of helping boys and girls achieve that life of excellence demanded not by the accomplishments of Russian science, not even by our American ideals, but by God himself. In the midst of this very proper emphasis, however, I am also uneasy. I do not want us to forget the fundamental job of education, which is to nurture human beings.

This is no easy assignment in view of the problems involved. An ever-increasing flood of young people expects and deserves an education. In the next fifteen years, secondary schools will enroll 75% more students than currently are enrolled. Colleges will enroll twice as many. In many areas of the country, schools are already overcrowded. What the future of education will be is difficult to imagine unless more buildings are erected quickly. Along with a shortage of buildings today is an acute teacher shortage. What of tomorrow? Colleges will need to add more teachers in the next ten years than had been added in their whole previous history. Fifty percent of all college graduates will have to enter teaching in the next ten years if even the present unsatisfactory student-teacher ratio is to be maintained.

Statements such as these are staggering, but they indicate only the quantitative side of the problem rather than the qualitative side, which is the really frightening aspect. The quality of teachers, of instruction, of education in general has been deteriorating steadily for some time. We know that frequently Johnny doesn't learn to read nor does his graduation from high school, or even from college, mean that he has received what was once meant by the term "good education."

Many — from professional educators to conspirators — have been blamed for this state of affairs. No one of us is either wholly guilty or wholly innocent. We in America have had a noble vision of education for all, but we have not realized its cost in terms of money, effort, and intelligence. Nor have we been prepared to pay the cost. We have preferred to erect superhighways, to produce and purchase multicolored cars, television sets, and air conditioners. These we have in abundance. Good education we do not yet have.

Education is not an abstract concept, however. It is made up of schools, boys, girls, people growing. And only as each of us in his particular community makes his own school stronger will the level of education in our nation rise. Our responsibility at St. Albans is to make St. Albans stronger, not only because we love the School but also because through so doing we can make our most important contribution toward strengthening education in America.

Last week I was reading a psalm in chapel when a verse seemed to rise out of the text with a meaning that I had never before known. It seems a rather curious verse at first sight: "Some trust in chariots and some in horses, but we will remember the name of the Lord our God." As I understand it, Psalm 20, from which the verse comes, was used by the ancient Hebrews before battle or in times of crisis to reaffirm their trust in God. This verse sums up the whole psalm. Some nations will put their trust in the size of their armies and in the strength of their equipment, but we will put our trust in the name, the character, and the spirit of the Lord our God.

That verse seems to speak directly to us today. In the modern idiom, I interpret the verse to mean: there are in these days of the cold war those who trust the number of our divisions, the size of our air force, or the stockpile of our atomic and hydrogen bombs, but we Christians will put our trust in the character of the Lord — in His understanding, His patience, His sympathy, His wisdom.

Given the kind of world we live in, it is evident that we must have our arsenals of bombs, atomic submarines, and jet planes. It would be wonderful if conditions were otherwise, but they are not. It is also evident, however, that we very much need to put our trust in a Force that expresses itself through gentleness, understanding, and love. For, if we are to live with people of all races and nationalities, we are more likely to be able to do so if we place our trust in the spirit of God, in His patience and justice, than if we place it completely in the force of our armaments, however powerful they may seem to be. Peace among men is most likely to come as we labor in His character, with His everlasting patience and mercy.

By educating our small group of boys, I believe that we at St. Albans can make a contribution to world peace. Perhaps more important, our graduates may be able to help solve some of the problems of education in general, such as those related to the quality of teachers, the nature of academic standards, the respect for hard work, the communication of values rooted in God.

Of course that is quite a job. But, then, we are always saying it is good for boys to be held to high standards and exacting requirements. And it is! Perhaps it is equally good for us. In your prayers, my friends, given thanks for these opportunities; roll up your sleeves, inform yourselves, give of yourselves. It it fun to have a job — especially a tough one.

Faithfully yours,

Charles Martin

O Lord Jesus, who attended the wedding feast and
who understands all the needs of man,
Grant us, we pray Thee, restraint in the pursuit
of all our pleasures.
And prevent us from the abuse of Thy manifold
gifts,
To the end that we may live joyously in Thy name.
Amen.

Ferdinand Ruge

XVI

The Use of Alcohol

December 8, 1958

Dear Friends,

I would like to consider with you the subject of drinking among our students. First let me say that drinking has been one of the least of my concerns at St. Albans. Rarely do I hear any complaints about our boys on this score. On the other hand, I don't hear all there is to hear! Then, too, I have lived long enough to know that alcohol gives a good many people trouble — whether they are young or old.

I am always proud of our boys at the parties we have here at St. Albans. I have never known any of our boys to appear at a dance or at any other School function having used alcohol. Such a fact is true partly because of the kind of boys they are and partly because they know we would not tolerate the use of alcohol. It is not merely I who would not tolerate it; it is the boys themselves. Drinking isn't part of the fabric of school life. I believe our life here is finer because of this attitude, and I wish our boys would carry that attitude to parties outside the School, to college, and into later life. I suppose — although it hadn't occurred to me until now — that I am writing this letter to convey my feeling that our boys would be finer, as would life itself, without alcohol and its abuses — even with its satisfactions.

In my experience, the young boy who takes a drink outside the home most often does so because he thinks it is "the thing to do," because he proves to himself and believes he proves to others that he is a man. Drinking makes him feel a bit wicked, attracts some attention, and provides him with a sense of recognition that he may have failed to receive in the normal routine of living.

When boys understand these motivations — and they generally do — they are likely to lay aside their foolishness. We all need approval and respect, particularly during that uncertain age known as adolescence. If a boy achieves recognition through the usual channels, he is less likely to seek it in unusual ways, either by drinking or by engaging in some other form of misbehavior. If he does not gain the recognition he needs, we as parents and schoolmasters can help him to find it. Further, we can show him that calling attention to himself by drinking is not the answer.

An older boy who drinks at parties may do so for the same reasons the younger lads do, but more often he may drink because he believes it is expected of him, because it seems the adult thing to do. It may be natural and fitting for our older students to drink, but I doubt it. There is always a high degree of self-consciousness in the schoolboy who, when he is out, drinks his beer or sips his cocktail. Such affectation, such false sophistication, clouds the healthy, vigorous young animal that is a young man. We tend to rush our young people into adult social patterns before they are ready. If a schoolboy is going to drink, I believe he can begin late rather than early.

No doubt some people will disagree with me about this matter. I have occasionally discovered that I am wrong. Some of our parents feel differently about high school drinking. And that's all right. I respect their judgment for their sons. I often hear, "We always have a cocktail at our home, and John is always free to have one. I believe it's better for him to learn to drink at home than elsewhere." Perhaps it is. I have often seen boys coming from this kind of home just as their parents would have them. But I have also occasionally seen lads who — through their behavior — belied such training. Of one thing I am very sure. You may serve a drink to your own son in your home; however, another boy — whose parents may have different ideas about alcohol — should not be served alcohol in your home. The state strongly forbids the public from selling or serving alcohol to minors.

This brings up another matter. Frequently a parent will say to me, "We had only a few bottles of beer. John just wouldn't have the party at the house if we didn't. He says all the boys have beer at their parties." I know it is easy to worry that if we don't allow drinking in our homes where we can supervise it, there is the danger that our boy will go elsewhere and drink — and that would be worse. It is difficult in this instance for parents to know what to do. Naturally John wants his party to be as sophisticated, as adult, as possible. However, the excuse that "everyone else does" should be questioned. My own feeling is strong: I believe that liquor should not be served at boys' parties.

One sometimes hears that a boy has taken liquor into someone else's home where none is served, or has sneaked to a car outside. To me, such an action is inexcusable. I can understand the action of a youngster who covets attention for himself. However, in my judgment, the attention that will do him the most good is the disapproval that comes from a heavy foot vigorously exercised to propel him out the door. He will appreciate such an action, for deep down he knows he deserves it.

It is not easy to write in terms of certainties and absolutes on any subject, particularly on this one, where customs are so varied and standards so confused. I suppose all of us would agree that the minimum we should expect of our boys is that, as they come to maturity, they should drink responsibly — some would say as gentlemen. The difficulty is, however, that we tend to sentimentalize and idealize the stereotyped picture of a gentlemen in terms of an unreal image of "gracious living." We forget or fail to focus upon the softness and excess, of the ungentlemanly conduct that often accompanies "gentlemanly drinking."

I would settle for a mature lad to whom alcohol was not a matter of overmuch concern and who drank mainly as a social grace. Still, I possess a streak of hardness, call it Puritanism, that causes me to prefer a boy not to drink at all. There is no high religious basis for this belief; I simply feel the average lad would be better off abstaining from alcohol. I am sure our world would be a better place for less, rather than more, drinking.

Whether we stand for moderation or for the Puritanism of the Headmaster, I am certain we all recognize that we must have standards and that our standards will not be met merely by expecting them or by demanding them of our boys. We shall have to provide them with standards and ideals expressed in our own lives. To do so is surely not easy; it requires help beyond ourselves. For that help and guidance, I commend you to that master whom we at St. Albans recognize as The Teacher, Jesus Christ, our Lord.

Faithfully yours,

Charles Martin

At a 1963 Book Fair: Columnist Art Buchwald, Charles Martin, and Mark Anthony.

"THE HOUSE DOG'S GRAVE" (HAIG, AN ENGLISH BULLDOG)

I've changed my ways a little; I cannot now
Run with you in the evenings along the shore,
Except in a kind of dream; and you, if you dream a moment,
You see me there.

So leave awhile the paw-marks on the front door
Where I used to scratch to go out or in,
And you'd soon open; leave on the kitchen floor
The marks of my drinking-pan.

I cannot lie by your fire as I used to do
On the warm stone,
Nor at the foot of your bed; no, all the nights through
I lie alone.

But your kind thought has laid me less than six feet
Outside your window where firelight so often plays,
And where you sit to read — and I fear often grieving for me —
Every night your lamplight lies on my place.

You, man and woman, live so long, it is hard
To think of you ever dying.
A little dog would get tired, living so long.
I hope that when you are living

Under the ground like me your lives will appear
As good and joyful as mine.
No, dears, that's too much hope: you are not so well cared for
As I have been.

And never have known the passionate undivided
Fidelities that I knew.
Your minds are perhaps too active, too many-sided . . .
But to me you were true.

You were never masters, but friends. I was your friend.
I loved you well, and was loved. Deep love endures
To the end and far past the end. If this is my end,
I am not lonely. I am not afraid. I am still yours.

*Robinson Jeffers**
*1887-1962***

**Submitted for the book by Stanley D. Willis, Class of 1946, English master and Director of Admissions at St. Albans School, 1955–1985.

XVII

Mark Anthony — I

September 11, 1959

Dear Friends,

I got a new dog. Mark Anthony is, at this writing, seven-and-a-half weeks old, born (appropriately) in St. Albans, Vermont, bred from champions. He is, of course, an English bulldog. Mark succeeds Cleopatra III, who died of a heart attack on graduation day. I had to wait a while before I could bring myself to find a successor to Cleo. When the time came for the decision, I chose a male after having had females for 25 years. It was easier that way. Since our females had all been Cleopatras, a male naturally had to be Mark Anthony. And so he is.

Mark Anthony is not aware of his importance. The world to him is a mass of objects to chew. But he *is* important. My family and I have learned much from our dogs. It may at times have been a bit rough on the dogs, but it has always been beneficial for us. Thanks to our dogs, I believe we are a more considerate, understanding, better disciplined, and finer family. You can't give yourself to something beyond yourself without becoming better in the process, because love — even love for an animal — enriches and blesses. Just as a family benefits from a dog, so, I believe, does a school. Cleo III was reserved, even shy. She did not enter largely into the life of St. Albans, but many of us observed in her a depth of response that shy people and creatures often bestow upon those who know them. Unlike Cleo, Mark Anthony seems hearty, outgoing, good-natured, and friendly. I expect that as he gradually learns the amenities of living, he will enter fully into our School life. Mark's headquarters are the Headmaster's Study.

Faithfully yours,

Charles Martin

Mark Anthony—II

January 24, 1962

Dear Friends,

This letter concerns Mark Anthony. You may remember that I mentioned my dog in an earlier letter. Two years ago, Mark was so small I could hold him in my hand. Today he is nearly full grown. Like all of us, Mark has known moments of glory and of disgrace. Now that he is a lusty, vigorous late adolescent moving into maturity — having gained some signs of good manners and good sense — I feel free to write about him. Although Mark is a dog, he has taught me much about boys and about life.

Mark Anthony loves life with the heartiness and enthusiasm of a vigorous 17-year-old St. Albans student. For him, there is no greater joy than to romp with a group of boys and chase a football or baseball or to clamp his jaws onto a strap and invite the world to wrestle it away from him. He loves to pit his strength against an opponent's. In a tug of war I have yet to see Mark's strength exhausted, but I have seen many of his antagonists cry for relief. Physical exercise is Mark's meat and drink. One can feel his exulting joy as he races about, throwing himself boldly into life.

Although Mark rushes headlong into all experiences with boundless energy and unrestrained curiosity, occasionally he suffers a rebuff. Physical rebuffs do not bother him, for his Creator endowed bulldogs with an imperviousness to pain. But being ignored, treated condescendingly, or disciplined unjustly — these acts hurt him just as they do humans. Occasionally I detect a loss of spontaneity or a quality of stubborn determination underneath his enthusiasm — just enough to show me that he is human. This is part of his growing process, so it does not disturb him or me. I foresee that it will be a long time before the harsh realities of the world cause his enthusiasm, interest, and curiosity to wane. I envy him that.

I must confess that I find his love of life particularly attractive. My every morning begins better because he emerges from his bed as I come downstairs and greets me with a sleepy but vigorous wiggling — not of his twist of a tail (which is incapable of wiggling) — but of his whole body. And I find it good to go home or to my study and receive a rousing welcome. His attention is not just occasional; it continues with troubled concern when I am preoccupied, with boisterous joy when I am active with him, and with constant, devoted companionship and affection always.

Though I welcome this companionship, it is not without problems. When an attractively dressed lady enters my study and is greeted with a physical effusiveness that would test the sturdiness of a field hand, I am somewhat embarrassed and not a little disturbed. There are times when Mark (like some humans I know) just does not have sense enough to be still and keep out of affairs that do not concern him. I would at times like to be free of the responsibilities he brings. I have performed more chores for him than I have for any of my children; his doctor bills are larger than those of other members of my family. However, these concerns don't trouble me because I know that life brings responsibility.

What does concern me is my occasional failure to bring under full control Mark's violent energy and boisterous curiosity. A boy just looked in. In spite of my command, Mark was all over the boy, acting as if the boy's only reason for entering my study was to see him. Even the use of my heel on Mark's toes when he jumped up on the lad merely caused a noisy romp around the room. Only after some battling did Mark finally quiet down. When we are out walking, a strange dog is sometimes more meaningful to Mark than my sharp command, "Heel." Still, such breaches of discipline do not bother me too much, for I see progress — even though it is slower than I should like!

Mark has taught me a valuable lesson: it is not always my will that should prevail. What is actually good discipline and my idea of good discipline sometimes differ. Mark's discipline problems stem largely from his inherent good qualities, qualities that are among the strengths of bulldogs. The high spirits and vigorous body that the Lord has endowed him with make it difficult for him to sit still or walk docilely. A genuine interest in everything, an unlimited affection for all people — these traits sometimes cause me irritation. The inborn stubbornness of the bulldog does not make for easy nurture or early control. As with children, it is wrong to expect maturity before years and experience permit it.

Mark can be downright cussed at times. He was born with his full measure of original sin. Each morning as I open the door of the car to go to school, he deliberately walks over to a bush or a post, sniffs at his own speed, and returns to the car when he is ready. Perhaps he senses my desire to hurry and rebels against it. I have tried many dodges to make him conform to my wishes, but he is either smarter or more tenacious than I, for the procedure is repeated each morning. I have come to believe that the act, calm and deliberate, is calculated to let me know I am his master because he wishes me to be. Furthermore, he wants me to know that he is independent. It is good to be reminded — even if by one's dog — that others have rights to be considered and respected.

Mark's feeding ritual constantly puzzles me; it also represents his need for independence. At first he appears eager. As I prepare his food, Mark solemnly watches the process. If I put the food outdoors, he remains in his bed for a measurable period. Deliberately he walks to the door and goes outside at his leisure. Having tried to explain this ritual to myself, I have come to the same conclusion that I have about the many puzzling habits and qualities of people: namely, that I just don't understand. Many of the behavioral and personality traits of my dog — as those of any human being — remain a mystery, however much I may try to understand them. Recognizing this fact does, I suppose, represent the beginning of wisdom.

Mark's mature personality is neither wholly what I expected it to be nor exactly what I would desire. I have never known any living creature to develop just as I thought he or she should. Nearly always I have expected too much; however, in my better moments I have realized that what I expected was not nearly as fine as what developed.

One aspect of Mark's growing up does, however, concern me. That is his tendency to take on the character of his master. I guess it is natural for any dog, as for any human being, to reflect the nature of those close to him. I would not mind if Mark reflected my strengths, but he seems to have a special affinity for mirroring my weaknesses. It would be nice if he were wiser, but of course that is true of his master as well. I do know that his master is wiser and better for having lived with him for two years — wiser, I hope, not only about dogs and about himself, but also about those other late adolescents with whom we are all so concerned — our boys.

Faithfully yours,

Charles Martin

Mark Anthony—III

November 26, 1963

Dear Friends,

Last night I took Mark Anthony for a walk. Preoccupied, I paid no attention to him, assuming that he was ambling behind me. He was not. He was plunging across the street, forcing a car to a sudden stop and heading straight for a couple who were standing on a lawn. Relieved that he had escaped traffic, I was also angry that he had broken discipline and bothered others. He came toward me, properly penitent. Unhappy that he had troubled me, Mark raced about nervously, listened to what I had to say, and followed at my heels for the remainder of the walk — more than usually attentive, obviously eager to make amends.

When I returned home, I mentioned the incident to my son, who usually takes Mark Anthony out at night. "He's stupid," said my son. This statement further annoyed me, for I don't like people to speak critically or thoughtlessly about my dog or, for that matter, about anything or anybody. Actually Mark Anthony is not stupid. To be sure, his action was thoughtless; like humans, however, dogs occasionally act thoughtlessly, even stupidly. By nature Mark is inquisitive, impetuous, and fearless; furthermore, he is the nosiest dog I have ever known. Anything new and different he must investigate. Even the commonplace represents a continuing source of curiosity and intrigue. Though such impetuosity is unusual in such a stolid breed of dog, the quality is pronounced in Mark. Interests are translated into immediate actions. Mark would not attack anything, but he responds with utter abandon when confronted by man, beast, or automobile. Even so, Mark's qualities must be accepted. The sooner we accept facts, the happier we are. I explained all this to my son. He remained unimpressed, but at least I felt better.

While to most people Mark's beauty is not obvious, he is handsome to his master and, like all bulldogs, devoted and gentle. The School has long grown accustomed to Mark, taking him for granted, save for the youngest boys to whom he is a continuing source of excitement and interest. In four years Mark has grown from a bundle of wrinkles and skin to a moderate-sized, fifty-pound dog. During that period, he has undergone many of the changes that humans undergo in a generation. Witnessing those changes firsthand has been helpful to me in understanding our boys.

Just as with the personality of a boy, so has the personality of Mark Anthony taken form as it moved from the self-centered, undisciplined playfulness of childhood through the rapidly changing, exuberant, uneasy period of adolescence into the individuality and maturity of adulthood. All this has been compressed into four years rather than into the twenty or more it takes for a human being to mature. Such an experience has been helpful to me in understanding boys.

Mark Anthony is basically the same dog he was when he was a pup. Human beings and dogs don't change radically as they age. Though they grow and mature, what was there to start with remains. Mark still has the strange habit that he had as a pup of getting under the tail of my coat as it hangs on the back of my chair or behind my cassock in the corner of the hall outside my study. Apparently this gives him a sense of security. He still loves to barrel around, testing his strength against that of anybody and anything. And people are still the joy of his heart. Yet in the sameness lies a difference.

As a pup, Mark went behind my cassock to rest and take in the sights from that vantage point. Anyone could tumble him out, and he would be off in a fit of play. Today nobody save myself or someone introduced by me can tumble him out. If they unwittingly approach my cassock in the corner, Mark growls in warning. He isn't unfriendly; in fact, he is as good-natured with people as ever. It is just that the cassock is mine and the corner is his.

Mark still loves exercise and play, but with a restraint he did not know when he was younger. He no longer forces himself on others. If a man wants to get some exercise and good sport, fine. If not, fine. He now understands that at times people are tired and have other interests, that they may not wish to romp and do what he wants to do. In this respect I find him more considerate than most humans. Often a boy insists that Mark play with a ball when he obviously has no desire to, but he goes along just to be accommodating.

There are times when Mark wishes to be alone. He has matured into an independent being, respecting others and expecting others to respect him. What dignity would any of us have if there were not lines beyond which others did not move and reserves that were ours alone or for the few with whom we cared to share them.

Mark is no longer given to wild demonstrations. He walks through our halls at School without a change of pace or movement of his head, even with a swarm of little boys pouring attention on him. At the bidding of a friendly man or woman he can remain immovable under my desk or even retreat to it. He has had his measure of rebuffs and no longer runs the risk of getting more. Even more important, he no longer needs to be the center of the world. He has had enough affection to feel secure, and he does not demand constant recognition and attention. The center of the world has moved from himself to others, chiefly to his master. Such changes are not unknown to humans.

As a result of his growing maturity, Mark has become a more pleasant companion. He often knows and understands my moods and thoughts more completely than I do. The plunge across that street would not have happened had I not been preoccupied, walking alone and in no real sense with him.

Like human beings, dogs grow to be uniquely themselves —

a composite of their genes and of those with whom they associate. Occasionally those selves are greater than the dreams their masters have for them, but those selves are always different. This is as it should be. Fortunately we cannot make, or remake, dogs or boys. We can but cooperate with One who knows more about making and remaking than we do.

Faithfully yours,

Charles Martin

O God, by whose Spirit we are led into the wilderness of trial: Grant that standing in Thy strength against the powers of darkness, we may so win the victory over all evil suggestions that with singleness of heart we may ever serve Thee, and Thee alone; through Him who was in all points tempted as we are, Thy Son Jesus Christ our Lord. Amen.

*John Wallace Suter**

---

*John Wallace Suter was a Dean of the Washington Cathedral from 1944 to 1950.

XVIII

Sex: An Attitude

February 9, 1960

Dear Friends,

This letter is about sex or, better yet, about an attitude toward it. During one of my dormitory rounds, I happened to notice on a bureau a small but prominently placed calendar of the cheese-cake variety — the kind with very attractive young ladies wearing little in the way of clothing. Deciding to check other rooms to see whether this was a common form of decoration, I saw only the usual pictures of sports heroes, family members, and the young ladies who so frequently need to be telephoned from School.

Next morning I talked to the calendar's owner. He was nonplussed by my concern. After all, weren't such calendars found everywhere? I agreed that they did appear in many places, but I said I preferred not to have them in my home on Woodley Road or in my other home, which is the School. After some discussion, he seemed to understand my viewpoint.

We rarely have problems at St. Albans that have to do with sex. On the whole, I find very little smut, vulgarity, or disturbance over the subject. I know that I don't hear and know all there is to hear and know, but I do feel I have been among boys long enough to make a fairly accurate judgment. There are fierce drives in all of us — especially in growing boys — that each of us must learn to live with. Occasionally I see the pain of these drives in the faces of some of our boys, but rarely am I distressed by what I see.

Sex is a central part of life, and it is difficult to overemphasize its importance, but we Americans succeed in placing too much emphasis on its physical aspects. If a man from outer space were to arrive among us in his spaceship and were to travel down Broadway at night, or were he to glance at our magazine covers in drugstores, look through the motion picture ads, or even read among contemporary books, he would surely come to believe that sex is the main concern of American life. While sex does represent an important aspect of living, it obviously does not encompass all of life.

Our extraordinary preoccupation with sex results from many factors. Chief among them, many agree, is a reaction against the prudishness of the past. We pride ourselves these days on being able to live openly with and talk frankly about the basic facts of life instead of hiding them or pretending that they do not exist — as was done in the benighted past. Also, we are told, modern psychiatry has brought sexual freedom to us by unveiling tortured inner areas of life and by freeing us from potentially explosive, dangerous repressions. While these explanations may be true, our present frankness and openness are so extreme that we must surely be ready for a counterreaction — one in which we learn to honor reserve, to respect privacy — even to stand in awe of what is, after all, sacred. There are parts of a man's life that are his and his alone, areas rarely to be shared with others and only then with a sense of reverence.

At a recent headmasters' meeting, a small group of men were discussing problems within their schools. One man was holding the floor on the subject of counseling, busily speaking of the importance of getting boys to talk, to open up, to lay bare their minds. I was not impressed. Healing often *does* come from being able to talk with someone who is warm and concerned, but I dislike probing and violating the sanctuary of a boy's inner self. I was happy to hear one headmaster say what has since remained with me: "I rarely do that. I think a boy's privacy has to be respected." With that, I agree. Certain private areas are sacred to individuals; these should be entered only by invitation and then only with great respect.

Parents are sometimes concerned about their inability to sit down with their sons and discuss openly the "facts of life." I can understand such inability; to me it is normal, even good. We ought not to be able to talk casually about the intimate. Sex in its highest form involves the noblest feelings we know. While the subject should be approached naturally, it should also be approached with respect, even with awe. I do not believe we need to create special occasions to talk about sex. Occasions will arise from the experience of being together. When they come, they can be met naturally but with respect for the thoughts, the inner life of a boy. Ultimately the attitude we desire for our boys will come from our attitudes, our example, and not through formal conversations or sex instruction, however well-intentioned such discussions may be.

At times I have considered the wisdom of offering a special course or of introducing into our regular curriculum material on the so-called "facts of life." I have always hesitated to do so. To me it has seemed more useful to present the facts of reproduction in the general science course in the Lower School, in biology in the Upper School, or in another course if the subject arises naturally. Because sex is a central issue in life, I do not believe the subject will be overlooked.

It is a common misconception that once the physical facts of sex are known, proper moral life will result. Such is clearly not the case. Only when a boy has the strength to govern his physical life, to live according to the highest standards we know, will a proper moral life result. One does not become a moral person through a course at school or talks at home, however important these may be, but through the values presented in the home and in the school.

One value I hold high is work. I am sure that an important reason why we seem to have little trouble at St. Albans with problems arising from sex is that our boys are kept busy with healthy, varied interests. I like to see a boy up to his chin in work, with books, with athletics, indeed, in any work in which he pursues his own special interest, whether it be art or music, automobiles or church. An active lad, extending himself fully in his work, is less apt to get into difficulty than one not so engaged.

As important as work is, however, there is a quality that transcends it and all other values, a quality rather uncommon among us. It is reverence — reverence that comes from appreciation of the sacred, for a recognition of the ultimate mystery of life. I felt that sense of wonder today when I picked up a very new baby and I did it — experienced hand that I am — hesitantly, fearfully, lovingly. It was what I knew a few days ago when I stood by a bedside and watched life ebb and death come.

This sense of awe, this recognition of mystery, this reverence for life is an ultimate value. We cannot have it for the asking. We cannot bequeath it or teach it to our boys, for it is not ours to give. Though it may be found in the home or in the school through example, it is a gift not from us but from God as we live humbly, openly, and receptively in relationship with Him.

When this sense of wonder comes to our boys, it will enable them to know that sex is the means through which God carries on the continuing and mysterious process of creation. Such respect will bring a reaction against the commonness and vulgarity with which sex is sometimes treated and create a respect for the body, for privacy, and for the awesome mystery of life.

All of which brings me back to where I began — calendar pictures. At one time, a common expression of art was the madonna — lovely, gentle, gracious, good. In our homes, in our lives, I would wish to see that conception of womanhood rather than the one found on the calendar or, alas, so generally among us. That picture of womanhood held high — the life the madonna reflects — is most apt to come when we and our children belong to that group, the Church, whose ultimate business is living together in harmony with the Holy One, whom we call God.

Faithfully yours,

Charles Martin

Let me use disappointments as material for patience.
Let me use success as material for thankfulness.
Let me use suspense as material for perseverance.
Let me use danger as material for courage.
Let me use reproach as material for long-suffering.
Let me use praise as material for humility.
Let me use pleasures as material for temperance.
Let me use pains as material for endurance.

*John Baillie**

**A Boy's Prayer Book*, p. 52.

XIX

The End of Your Rope

April 4, 1960

Dear Friends,

What do you do when you reach the end of your rope? What do you do when you have tried every approach, sought every imaginable way out of difficulty and you seem to get nowhere? What do you do when all seems futile and foolish; when you have worked hard, done your best, struggled on and on, and still feel you can hold on no longer? What do you do when you get to the end of your rope?

Driving along R Street this morning, I saw Alex, who had attended St. Albans several years previously. He told me that he had just quit his job and was looking forward to attending college. There was pride and conviction as he spoke of his plans.

At St. Albans, Alex had been a nice enough boy, but he had rarely passed his course work, requiring tutoring or summer sessions to improve his grades. Though he was never involved in serious trouble, he was never without petty, annoying problems. His parents had been ambitious for their son, giving him everything they could, and they gave him much. However much they gave, though, it was put aside unused or slipped away unappreciated. I used to marvel at their patience. Occasionally the father would explode in exasperation, but he always subsided, bearing failure with endurance, with patience.

Together we strove to find answers to help Alex — compulsory study halls, shortened weekends, special work, threats, cajolery. Alex did what was expected after a fashion, but nothing happened. Since St. Albans was not helping Alex, at our suggestion he went to a different school. After moving from school to school, he entered the military service. The last time I saw his parents, they admitted no despair. Rather, they hoped against hope that their boy would somehow "make good."

Now all had changed. Alex had done some radio work while in the army. After leaving the service, he had gotten a job with a radio station. He had apparently done well. I could understand his success, for Alex was easy of speech and was gifted with a warm, friendly manner that carried conviction. It seemed that Alex had found an interest; his talents in this area had brought him substantial success. He would attend college, but he would continue to work at his love, radio. One could feel the sense of purpose in the man.

I could not help but remember his parents' willingness to carry on when most of us would have given up. Although they did not possess the understanding to help Alex find himself at school (and neither did I), they did have the patience to remain with him until he did. As I think about boys who have had problems, I see many who had to keep plugging, to wait until the moment in their development when something was kindled within them or until circumstances came together in just that complex of events necessary to their finding themselves. No force, no worry, no wisdom had seemed adequate to help — staying power had been the only answer.

A man left my study this afternoon. I saw him to his car, fearful that he would not make it, for he was crippled and had crutches that seemed taller than I. This great, hulking man had to back up the steps of the terrace, get into the car by an elaborate process that involved his unfastening braces, lifting each leg, and locking braces. I remember that man as a boy when polio hit him. And I remember the suffering of his parents. I was with them through much of their agony.

Stunned at first, his mother had carried on as if she were in a trance. There was a long period during which she was with her son constantly, a time when we feared more for her than for him. He accepted his illness — as boys so often do — as a natural part of living. While the boy made some progress, his mother became worn physically as well as hard and embittered. Why had this happened to her boy? What kind of future could he look forward to? How could she go on?

Then she changed. Understanding, gentleness, and great strength came to her. In spirit she carried both her son and her husband. To know her was to be lifted up. The change, she has told me, took place when she was able to accept the tragedy, accept her son's handicap, accept life as it was. She had battled, gone on when the odds against her had seemed impossible. Finally — she did not know how or why — she had ceased to fight, to deny the facts. By accepting things as they were, she came to know peace, and others knew peace through her.

A friend of mine was having a tough time. His wife was not able to cope with the daily problems of living. Each day he went off to work worried about her condition, concerned about the children. Rarely was there a day during which he was not summoned to come home; rarely was the trouble serious, but there was always upset. My friend tried every measure, or so he thought — medical and psychiatric help, rest, change, vacation, hospitalization, return to family. None of these measures appeared to help. We talked often, and I frequently feared more for my friend's sanity than for that of his wife. It seemed as though he could not carry on much longer.

Then one day someone came along, took my friend's wife by the hand, and found her a job. Why I or the skilled professionals so often consulted did not suggest the idea, I do not know. I do know that for the moment my friend's wife knows peace and so does her family. It has been as simple as that.

So often we go along searching for profound, hidden answers. Then when we think we have tried everything and all looks hopeless, there comes an answer so simple, so obvious, that its very simplicity apparently made it difficult to discern.

What do you do when you reach the end of your rope, when

all seems bleak and hopeless, even though you have done your best? You keep right on going. And somehow out of the hopelessness and the despair come light and hope. Hope may come unexpectedly and simply as to my friend; more often, hope comes through an understanding and acceptance of things as they are — from a wisdom greater than ours — in a time beyond our determining. This is in the very nature of living. The season of the year through which we are passing — Eastertide — proclaims this message.

The Teacher whom men call Jesus Christ was brought to death by the forces of expediency, indifference, self-will, and self-righteousness. To His disciples on the first Good Friday, those forces of evil seemed to have triumphed over goodness. All seemed lost, hopeless. He whom they loved and trusted, in whom was their life and their hope, had died. They were a beaten, despairing group. Then, one by one, they came to know — each in his own way — that their Teacher was still with them even unto the end of the world. In the strength of that conviction they set forth to spread that good news abroad. They and their friends went even unto the uttermost ends of the earth to proclaim the message that however much evil may seem to triumph, goodness will eventually vanquish it.

One who had learned of the Teacher and who had known Him through a moving experience that had transformed his own life, wrote in a letter, "All things work together for good to them that love God, to them who are called according to *His* purpose." To those of us who seek to know and to do God's will, who do the best we know how in His spirit, somehow or other our life works out for the good. Though we may not escape trouble and adversity, we do learn to bear it and to grow in wisdom and in understanding through our experiences, and life becomes good. The results may not be as we had planned or expected; the route may be long and circuitous, with unexpected twists and turns. Yet I believe the words of St. Paul. In my heart I know the lesson of the gospel.

We can go on when it is difficult to do so, sure in the hope that a way out will come, confident that we shall have the strength to bear whatever the trouble is, certain that we can surmount, even triumph over, our problems. At the heart of life is Goodness, is God. Through Him and His enduring love, evil is conquered.

What do you do when you come to the end of your rope? What do you do when life overwhelms hope and brings despair? Why, you keep on going, sure in the hope and certain in the conviction that God and God's love within us will overcome the world.

Faithfully yours,

Charles Martin

O God, Who dost turn the hearts of the fathers unto the children and has granted unto youth the grace to see visions and unto older persons the grace to reflect; we beseech Thee to draw together the old and the young, that in fellowship with Thee they may understand and help one another and in Thy service find their perfect freedom, through Jesus Christ our Lord. Amen.

Charles Martin

XX

Youth and Age

May 24, 1961

Dear Friends,

This letter, while it does not directly address the varied life of the School, does — in a larger sense — address an issue that warrants our attention. That issue is the relationship of old persons and young persons and the need each has for the other.

Most of us know something about older people's problems from direct experience with family members or close friends. These concerns are many, real, often tragic. However, too much discussion and worry can cause a self-consciousness in older persons that breeds unnecessary fears, insecurities, and difficulties where none might otherwise have existed. Life consists of problems. We would all be healthier, less anxious, and more secure if we recognized this fact, accepted it, and worried less.

I want to think with you briefly about the common needs of both young and old people. Physical concerns — health, housing, insurance, economic security, these receive the greatest attention. Yet, even if they were solved, the greatest need would still be left unanswered. It is of little use to help people live, no matter how comfortably, if their lives have no purpose, no meaning. One does not truly live if, after retirement, all one has to do is sit on a park bench or a rocking chair. Nor is it living if, after raising one's family, one remains on the sidelines, idly watching life pass by. The most important need of older people, of younger people, indeed of all human beings, is to know a sense of being wanted, needed, and valued. An older person wants to feel part of a group and necessary to it.

This intrinsic need can most naturally be met for all of us through the family. A family benefits from the stability, wisdom, and quietness of older persons; on the other hand, it also is made richer by the vigor, enthusiasm, and high spirits of youth. Modern difficulties of living sometimes obscure the ever-present need we have for each other, particularly that which the young have for the old.

Recently, I was visiting in a home where there lived two boys, their parents, and a very old lady — a great aunt. Because the great aunt was quite frail, she required much care. It was obvious she received such care and was very much part of the family. In answer to my question about the way the family accepted the responsibility of the great aunt, I was told, "She needs much care and it has been difficult at times, but it has been very good for all of us. It has been good for the boys to have to think of someone else. They have learned to be much more sensitive, thoughtful, and considerate." I could see the sacrifice that the frail old lady cost the family, but it was good to realize the gifts she had brought to them: a sense of responsibility, sensitivity, and gentleness.

From the time he retired until his death, "Pop" Henderson, our greatly loved chaplain emeritus, conducted chapel one evening every week. "Pop" had about him the deliberateness that often comes with age; there were periods of heavy silence while he thumbed his way about in the prayer book and Bible. At first I was fearful lest our boys would be restless and inconsiderate, that "Pop" would be disturbed, perhaps hurt. But the boys were even more attentive than at other evening services. They were obviously impressed not only by the service but also by "Pop." His white hair, benign square-jawed face, and deliberate movements gave "Pop" a dignity of person, wisdom, and strength that spoke compellingly to us all.

A few days ago I visited one of our parents confined to her home following an operation. Her mother, who lived nearby, had moved over to her daugther's home for the duration of the emergency. "I don't know how we could get along without Mother," my convalescent parent observed. "Mother holds the fort whenever we need her. We always seem to need her."

Some time ago, an article in *The New York Times Magazine* addressed the need for grandparents in suburbia. Its point: most suburbs teem with children whose young parents are unable to cope with them and simultaneously with the problems of the home. The wisdom and help of older persons are necessary but are rarely present. Most young parents require not only the physical help that their parents can give but also the wisdom of the previous generation to meet life.

For years we had a grandfather who brought several of his young grandchildren to our athletic contests. He enjoyed athletics, but, more important, he enjoyed his grandchildren and they enjoyed him. I liked to watch the children, ice cream cones in hand, climb in and out of the grandstand and occasionally engage in their own vigorous games. I was always reminded of my own grandparents — of the fun I had with them, the stories they told me about my parents, the "olden days" they revealed, and the continuity of life they communicated.

My observation is that grandparents enjoy their young grandchildren with a naturalness and freedom from strain that most parents cannot. I suppose that it is partly because grandparents do not have the continuing, wearing care and the ultimate responsibility. They can safely enjoy, even spoil. It is good for children and grandparents to share one another's company.

I realize that not all older people are gentle, gracious, white-haired souls who are easy to live with and who bless us just by their very presence. Neither are we all the sweet-tempered persons we may appear to be. We have to accept each other for what we are and love each other in spite of and because of what we are.

A fundamental truth at the heart of Christian living is that we are dependent upon one another. The lives of all of us are poorer without interaction among young, middle-aged, and older people.

As we learn to worship the Lord our God with all our heart and soul and mind, we will come to live out the commandment

— honor thy father and thy mother. As we give ourselves to compassion, wisdom, righteousness, and love, the grace of God, working in and through us, may enable us and our society to live together in mutual helpfulness.

Faithfully yours,

Charles Martin

Charles Martin takes a swing with the baseball team and . . . mingles with the crowd at a football game, 1960's.

Lord, help us to be the masters of ourselves, to say "no" sometimes so that we may be the servants of others. Take our eyes and help us to see, take our ears and help us to listen, take our mouths and speak through them, take our hearts and set them on fire with love of your Son, our Savior, Jesus Christ. Amen.

*Roger Bowen**

---

*The Reverend Roger Bowen is Chaplain at St. Albans School, having served from 1973 to 1976 and from 1982 to the present.

XXI

And the Lord Said "NO"

November 17, 1961

Dear Friends,

Over her living room doorway, Dr. Adelaide Case (the first woman to become a professor at an Episcopal Seminary) had hung a huge framed text, "And the Lord said ' No.' " Visiting this gracious, friendly lady for the first time, I was surpised to find such a strangely negative text in her home. I could not resist asking the why of it. Explained Miss Case: "I find it very difficult to refuse anyone, and I need to be reminded continually that sometimes one must say ' No!' "

Like Miss Case — and like most of us, I suppose — I seldom find it easy to say "No." If someone asks me to speak on an occasion six months away, I say "Yes" almost without hesitation. Only when the occasion is a week away and I am swamped with responsibilities do I ask myself in wonder, "Martin, why did you ever take that on?"

The same holds true in my relations with St. Albans boys. If a boy asks, "Sir, may I do so-and-so?", I almost automatically say "Yes." It is so much easier and more pleasant that way. A "Yes" involves neither the labor of making a decision nor the pain of causing hurt. A "No" may cause disappointment and discomfort, and no one enjoys having to cause either.

Every parent at times finds it difficult to say "No." One prefers to be amiable, to keep peace in the family. Like Miss Case, however, we must realize that a good, strong, positive "No" has its place in the nature of things. Occasionally parents seek my assistance in getting other parents to agree about how to cope with the common social problems of young people: late hours, cars, alcoholic beverages. It is true that a cooperative approach is often helpful. But a group approach can never furnish a complete solution to these problems.

We live during a time when standards vary. It is difficult for a group to agree on desirable standards; moreover, it is difficult to observe those standards. Responsibility for behavior must rest, finally, with the individual. The individual, not the group, must say "Yes" or "No."

In the classroom, a new master has to learn to handle his class by himself. Interference by the School would remove the master's authority and make it impossible for him to carry on. He is the only one who can enforce discipline in his classroom. He must develop the ability to say "No" and have the authority within himself to give that "No" reality.

Ultimately, the behavior of our sons is determined by their parents' standards of behavior and authority. Parents themselves must be able to say "No." Any intrusion of authority from outside the home, any removal of authority from the parents, is just as destructive to the discipline and order of the home as is the removal of authority from a teacher in his classroom.

It may be helpful for us to remember that those who work with young people have found that individuals do not suffer from having parents who have been too severe or from parents who have said "No" too often. On the contrary, young people suffer from indecisiveness and from the lack of authority so prevalent in our time. All of us need limits.

A wise and kindly bishop once told me, "The responsibility that is the hardest for me to bear is having to say 'No.' One must have the capacity to hurt." I understood what he meant. Whether one is head of a church, school, or family, he must be able to say "No" when he believes he is right, even though he may hurt those with whom he is associated and whom he dearly loves. Saying "No" to a long-planned big weekend and having to deal with the unhappiness of a boy — uncertain whether you have been right in your judgment — is not easy. To hold to that "No" takes a stronger character than is natural to most of us. Sometimes we refuse our boy because we want to enable him to learn from painful — even bitter — experience.

Last spring for my Sacred Studies course I required that my students read *Letters from a Headmaster's Study.* Running no chance of its being unread, I assigned it to two boys whose judgment I respected, boys who would have courage to say what they liked and disliked about the book. Independently, they both agreed that the letter they most liked was the one entitled "Love That Suffereth Long." As its central theme, this letter makes the point that a boy should be allowed to experience the consequences of his own actions. Both boys recognized that young people (I would say all people) need to learn this way. Neither of the boys, I believe, recognized the quality of love on their parents' part that makes such a course possible. There is no love greater. The "No" that permits a boy to learn from painful experience takes great courage and love.

Finally, I do not mean to suggest that one must go about with a petulant and unsympathetic "No" always on his lips. I do mean that it is not enough for us merely to be amiable, good-natured, well-intentioned parents. We must have firm convictions that mean enough to us to enable us to say "No" regardless of what anyone else says or does, regardless of how much it may temporarily hurt those whom we most love.

I tend to err on the side of softness myself. Thus, I find it helpful to remember the text over Miss Case's door: "And the Lord said 'No.' "

Faithfully yours,

Charles Martin

Teach us, good Lord,
To serve Thee as Thou deservest;
To give, and not to count the cost;
To fight, and not to heed the wounds;
To toil, and not to seek for rest;
To labor, and not to ask for any reward
Save that of knowing that we do Thy will.

St. Ignatius of Loyola

XXII

Life Is Not Easy

January 5, 1962

Dear Friends,

Occasionally before a vacation period I receive a request to excuse a boy a day or two early or to extend his vacation by a few days. Usually the request seems reasonable — the only chance for the family to go off together, a special invitation that will not come again, a wonderful opportunity for a boy to learn through travel. I always explain carefully that I understand and appreciate the reason behind the request. And I do. But I nearly always say that I cannot grant the request. I make the point that if I excuse one boy I must excuse another. And that is impossible, for the opening and closing of school would be so ragged that we could not operate. Schools cannot work with conviction and character if they limp along as they open or peter out as they close.

When time permits, I explain something that is even more important to me. If a boy and his family deny themselves the pleasure of an attractive holiday or an extra day or two of vacation, the lad learns a lesson far more valuable to him than having a few extra days of fun. It is then plain to him that school is very important. The act says more than much talking. It is natural to exhort a boy to study when he is not doing well. It is easy to scold him when he doesn't seem to be putting forth enough effort. It is comforting to oneself to speak about the importance of a good education. However, what really speaks to a boy is putting education ahead of pleasure, whatever the cost or inconvenience to ourselves.

Before a vacation I go over all this with our boys, closing with, "I shall be grateful if you don't request special permission, because I dislike saying no to any request, especially those made by you. These requests always seem reasonable, but I just can't say yes to them. Therefore, I shall appreciate it if you do not ask me to say what I don't want to say and what you don't want to hear. It will save us both embarrassment." Being fine boys, they usually understand.

Lateness I also take seriously. At the risk of being considered old-fashioned, I believe that it is important to be on time in good weather and in bad weather, any time and all the time. We owe it to others. We owe it to ourselves.

I can understand a boy's being late occasionally, very occasionally. Unavoidable accidents occur, but the unavoidable is often avoidable if one employs foresight and effort. If there is a bad storm, we shall have to start from home earlier. If traffic is uncertain, we must allow a greater margin of safety. But whatever the unavoidable means, we must be prepared. School takes precedence over comfort and convenience. School is a primary obligation.

Incidentally, it is interesting to observe that our records show that lateness has little to do with distance from school or with difficulty of travel. It has to do with mental attitudes. The boy who lives nearby is as likely to be late as the boy who lives thirty miles away.

I try to make clear that I do not believe we can hole up and escape difficulty when it comes along in life. This goes for bad weather, bad times, bad anything. Our job in life is not merely to adjust to what life brings us but to meet and try to overcome it. When adversity comes we must dig ourselves out, just as we would get up early to dig our car out of the snow.

Recently a book came to my attention entitled *Science Made Easy*. I got rid of it in a hurry, but the title has stayed in my mind to plague me. The idea of things being made easy represents so much of what is wrong with modern education and modern life that I cannot easily forget it. Science cannot be made easy; it is an exacting discipline that demands all there is in man. It ought to be presented with all its interest and wonder, with its opportunity to know and to appreciate, but never as something easy. What satisfaction comes from doing the easy?

Life is not easy. To believe otherwise is to contradict experience and to delude ourselves. It is natural for parents to seek to spare their children as many difficulties and hurts as possible. It is natural and right for teachers to help students through painful periods of learning and growth, but often it seems the emphasis is so great on sparing and making things easy that we fail to prepare our children for the realities of life.

At St. Albans I want our boys held to the highest that is in them. I don't want boys expected to do the impossible, but I do want them to know the challenge of doing hard work, the discipline of missing and trying again, the experience of being extended to the limit, and the satisfaction of meeting the difficult and overcoming it. If we err at St. Albans — and I hope we don't err too often — I want it to be on the side of expecting too much rather than too little.

This past weekend I saw a basketball game, a wrestling tournament, and a soccer match. This sounds like a good deal of athletics, but I loved it. It was good to see the boys enjoy their successes; it was good to see them experience failures. I like St. Albans to win games, but I don't mind our losing as long as we have played our best. While nearly all our boys do their best, sometimes there is one not willing or able to discipline himself, one who refuses to pay the price of success. He is not able to lay aside the easy and pleasant for the unpleasant and difficult. He is unable to make the necessary effort to meet his responsibilities when it is comfortable not to do so. That kind of lad is rarely aware of these shortcomings. Wanting always to win, when he does not he finds something in the other team or in the circumstances that enables him to rationalize his failures so that he can be at peace with himself.

One of the difficulties in helping such a boy recognize his problem is that he doesn't realize that "a man is made of one piece." We cannot work hard or train with sacrifice for a game — we cannot give our best — if we are not in the habit of working hard and training for every aspect of life. One must have an attitude toward life that enables him to meet the unpleasant and difficult with courage and vigor, an attitude that enables him to meet the seemingly unimportant demands of life, from promptness in assignments and appointments, to missing a movie or a vacation, with a straightforward sense of responsibility. A boy cannot have the will to win in sports if he does not have it in every aspect of life. He is "made of one piece" and, although he may deceive himself, he cannot be soft and self-indulgent in one area of life while being tough and disciplined in another. We must help him to learn this fact if he is to be free to face and solve his problems.

American life is, on the whole, comfortable, easy, even luxurious. We whose sons are at St. Albans are more able than many to share in life's comforts. We can give our children more, spare them more, protect them more. For that very reason we must be forever on guard against sparing them too much and failing to give them the strength they need to meet the realities that are hard, demanding, even tragic at times. We must help our boys not by exhortation, but by precept and example. We must help them not alone in the moment of trouble, but in a continuing attitude toward life that will enable them in little things, as well as in great things, to face the realities of life not with softness but with courage and firm conviction.

Faithfully yours,

Charles Martin

Almighty God, who hast revealed Thyself as the Word Incarnate and hast bestowed on us the gift of language; grant that in our words we may always seek to speak the truth in love and neither confuse others nor shirk our responsibilities. We ask this in the name of Thy Word of Love, Jesus Christ our Lord. Amen.

*Robert Cain**

*The Reverend Robert Cain served St. Albans as Upper School Chaplain and teacher from 1979 to 1985.

XXIII

A Spade Is a Spade

November 8, 1962

Dear Friends,

For weeks the phrase "A spade is a spade" has been echoing through my mind. Recently, a psychiatrist spoke to me about a man who had visited both of us. Said the psychiatrist, "He is selfish and he is a coward. He does what he does because he wants to." I was surprised not only by the doctor's comment but also by the force with which he (a quiet, self-restrained doctor) expressed it. The statement was accurate, however, and I understood his exasperation. As a matter of fact, it was so good to hear a spade called a spade that the statement has been intruding itself into my mind ever since.

Most of us habitually use circumlocutions to say things politely and to avoid giving offense. At a baseball game the official announces over the public address system: "Anyone reaching onto the playing area or moving onto it to get a baseball will be escorted from the park." The official means: "The person will be thrown out." A master writes in a report: "He is a nice boy with many gifts, but he has not yet learned to use his full potential." The teacher means: "The boy is able, but he is failing because he is lazy. He needs to learn self-discipline or he will continue to fail."

By their very nature euphemisms are seldom clear; likewise,

they are neither forceful, direct, nor completely honest. Worse, they tend to breed thinking habits that evade truth and place responsibility not where it should be placed, but elsewhere. Isn't it far better to call a spade a spade?

I am well aware that one needs to speak and write in a pleasing manner to win people rather than cause them to be resentful or to close their minds. I also know how desperately we all need compassion, understanding, and love. But I know, too, that one must be honest, definite, and responsible. Much harm can be done in the name of love by a kind of softness so fearful of hurting that it evades speaking the truth. By being less than honest, by sugar-coating our statements, we are not only being unkind to persons we want to reach and to help, but we are also avoiding responsibility.

A recent report on juvenile delinquency contained the following observations about taking vs. evading personal responsibility. The writer observed that juveniles in England, when asked about the reasons for their troubles, gave answers like: "Aw, I bashed him on the head, " "I swiped some money," or "I had a little joyride in a car and smashed it up." Some of the questions asked of young people in juvenile courts in our own country brought answers like: "They never gave me a chance," "My friend squealed on me," "My social worker fouled me up," or "They gave me a punk for a lawyer." The English group recognized personal responsibility; the American group shifted responsibility. Significantly, the writer reported that when responsibility is placed squarely upon the individual, social workers appear to have more success in dealing with the juveniles involved.

Among ourselves at School I sometimes see this tendency to "pass the buck." A master says of a boy: "He will not work" or "He shows no interest." Why will he not work? Why is he not interested? We seek reasons in ourselves, in the home situation, in his adolescent adjustment. Sometimes we find reasons; sometimes we do not. Often, in our earnest desire to uncover a reason, we fail to recognize an obvious fact—the boy himself has failed to accept his responsibilities.

As I write this letter, I am reminded of the persistent effort the faculty made to understand a boy. We had long talks with him, with his friends. Finally we arrived at a composite picture of a shy boy, overawed by the successes of those around him—a boy given to escape into the security of what he can do easily. With this understanding, we went to work. Nothing happened. Then out of the blue came an experience that jolted him into new life. A teacher wiser than the rest of us said with iron authority, "You *must*," and the boy *did*. Our concern and sympathy were beneficial, even necessary, but we did not find a solution. The methods that ultimately worked in this case were the master's direct approach and the boy's acceptance of his responsibility.

Occasionally we hear such excuses as "Mom can't spell either, and I guess that's why I can't," or "Dad flunked freshman math so I guess it runs in the family." Such statements may contain a measure of truth; more likely, they are rationalizations that afford an easy avenue of escape from personal responsibility, permitting a boy to accept a situation that need not be accepted. Hard work and a refusal to accept defeat will usually enable a boy—or any of us, for that matter—not only to do the possible, but often to achieve the impossible.

All of this makes me somewhat uncomfortable. By nature, I am one who seeks constantly to understand, to sympathize with, and to avoid saying or doing what may hurt. I am too much given to euphemisms and circumlocutions. Yet I know that unless controlled and wisely directed, the efforts involved in avoiding hurt may defeat their own purposes. The spirit of our times to "pass the buck" from ourselves to others or to society—to any cause beyond our control—resists calling a spade a spade, resists straightforward acceptance of our responsibilities.

The parable of The Prodigal Son speaks about such honesty.

> I will arise and will go unto my father and say unto him, father, I have sinned against Heaven and in thy sight and am no more worthy to be called thy son . . . . It was meet that we should make merry and be glad; for this thy brother was dead and is alive again; and was lost and is found.

Beautiful as is the language, infinitely more important is what the Gospel says. At the heart of the world is goodness—the goodness of forgiving and sustaining love. As soon as we can recognize that we have been less than our best, that we have not taken personal responsibility—as soon as we can call a spade a spade—we will receive the grace to discover a new life. We who were dead can be reborn.

Faithfully yours,

Charles Martin

Lord, as we prepare to serve Thee by applying for admission to colleges, help us to avoid tensions and anxieties that warp perspectives; help us further to pursue and to accept not simply what fashion dictates but that which will best ready us to do Thy will; and, above all, help us to remember that striving and learning, uninformed by love, have no meaning.

This we ask in the name of Thy Son, Jesus Christ, whose wisdom and love know no bounds. Amen.

*John F. McCune**

*John F. McCune is Assistant Headmaster of the Upper School at St. Albans.

XXIV

Admission to College

April 16, 1963

Dear Friends,

After a recent meeting of our Fifth Form parents, I was troubled. Although there had been pleasant visits and helpful conversations about our boys, we had failed in our primary aim: to foster better understanding about the next step in our boys' education—admission to college. At the meeting, our discussion had centered upon the mechanics involved in college placement—when and how to apply. What we had not done was to place college entrance in its proper perspective. Consequently the meeting produced an aggravation rather than an alleviation of parental anxieties.

Getting into college has become, unfortunately, a matter of worrisome concern so general that newspapers editorialize about the subject, magazine articles are written about it, and TV and radio programs address the issue. Some schools make college entrance—or so it seems—their sole reason for existence. For many students, the last year of secondary school—even all the years of secondary school—have become a period of anxiety and tension. As a result, it is perhaps inevitable that parents and students confronted with the problem of college placement are at once bewildered and apprehensive.

Such concern is not to be wondered at, for a college education is perhaps more important today than at any other time in our history. To be sure, a college education *can* be the key to the world of comfortable income and secure social position; however, it is *not* the key to the Kingdom of Heaven nor is it even the key to a good life. Quite the contrary, as a college education is pursued by some and perverted by others, it can become a handicap to living a good life and a stumbling block to gaining the Kingdom of Heaven.

The first step toward placing college admission in its proper perspective is, paradoxically, to realize that our most important job as parents and schoolmasters is to try *not* to get our boys into college. Rather, our aim should be to nurture boys so that their innate abilities and potentialities are fully developed, their curiosity and interests healthfully stimulated. Our job is to prepare boys to live happily and productively among their fellows and with their environment.

At. St. Albans we take it for granted that our boys will go to college, and that is fitting. We have always been and we are likely to remain a college preparatory school. Still, this does not mean that we must give undue concern to college admission. To do so would resemble the unhealthy concern an occasional boy has about grades. Although we like our boys to get good marks, we do not want them to work toward that end alone. Instead, we want them to have the fun of pursuing a subject for its inherent interest, to have the pleasure of experiencing the satisfaction of high achievement for its own sake. Any grade should be incidental to the stimulation of intellectual curiosity. Likewise, attending college should ideally be an incidental result—the natural next step to a secondary education filled with the satisfaction of hard work and of academic achievement. At St. Albans we do not want parents and boys to worry about college admissions. We want to be concerned with giving boys a sound education; the future will then take care of itself.

Another mistake we commonly make was perfectly illustrated by an occurrence in one of my Sixth Form classes. When I arrived in the Trophy Room, there was an unnatural quiet save for the music of a piano. A boy was playing, and the class was lost in rapt attention. As I joined the listeners, the period flew by and passed without the boys having to be exposed to the wisdom of the Headmaster. They were little the worse for that experience and much better for having listened to the music. The Headmaster, too, left feeling refreshed. Yet he was disturbed by a question. What could the bookish education that both St. Albans and the usual college provide contribute to this talented pianist? Though such an education could broaden his understanding and presumably enhance his personality, it could also take too much time and energy away from the development of his remarkable gifts. In our preoccupation with getting our sons into college and with the pressures we put upon them to succeed, we fail to encourage gifts that some colleges cannot, or at least do not, recognize for admission or nurture once the boy has been admitted. Thus we narrow the lives of boys and leave all life the poorer.

Still another evil common among us is the emphasis placed upon college entrance examinations and our failure to understand their limitations. Testing agencies have developed examinations that, within limits, are useful tools for measuring ability and achievement. No test, however, can accurately measure specific ability, much less the mystery of the human personality. Different or unusual talents will, of course, escape measurement in group tests.

College Board scores are not absolutes. The great importance that parents, schoolmasters, and colleges attach to these measurements gives them such an inordinately important role in the minds of students that a boy who doesn't perform well in these mass tests often begins to view himself as a failure as a student and as a person. A fine boy is sometimes permanently handicapped, failing to make his unique contribution to life because such tests and the importance we place upon them have given him a distorted view of himself. College entrance examinations can be useful provided we are conscious of their limitations; however, excessive emphasis and reliance on them frequently negate their value and can even cause harm.

As evil as the emphasis on mass tests is the emphasis on admission to a "prestige" college. It is unwise to make up one's mind in advance that Johnny should attend the "University of Ivy

League" because a relative went there or because it is "the place to go." Indeed, these colleges are wonderful, but so are a hundred other colleges. Some boys can best develop in a small college; others will do well in a large university. Still others may do best in a technical school.

Watch your boy as he grows; visit some colleges with him; meet with his college advisor. Then, choosing with understanding, apply to colleges where your boy will best continue to grow. In making a choice, consider many factors but keep an openness of mind that will encourage your boy and make him eager to take full advantage of opportunities wherever he goes.

There is no one "good" college for a boy; indeed, there are many fine ones. More important than the quality of a college is the keenness of desire, the willingness to struggle, the openness of mind with which a student goes to college. A good education—the knowledge of goodness, the knowledge of God himself—comes not from any environment, however good, but rather from a willingness to work and a deep desire to understand and to know.

Today, of course, colleges are having far more applicants than they can accept; this trend promises to continue. The plain fact is that competition is a lot tougher than when you and I entered college. I frequently thank the good Lord that I received my formal education when I did, for I doubt whether I could make the grade today. When I see the work piling up at St. Albans, I sometimes wonder whether I could have graduated from here! And that is good. It is only when competition is keen, when stresses and strains are great, that the finest is elicited from any of us.

But enough of this. College admission with all its pressures is a fact of life. Pressures in themselves are not bad. We can grow strong under pressure. What we need to do is learn to bear pressures that are wise, right, and unavoidable, and to eliminate those that are not. But most important, we need to have a clear understanding of what we are trying to do for our boys.

The end of education is to enable our boys—and ourselves—to live usefully, richly, fully—today and every day. This purpose, worked at earnestly, patiently, and humbly, in the spirit of the

Teacher Jesus Christ, who has done some unusual things with human beings, will allow us to see college admission and all the impedimenta of living in their proper perspective. This perspective will come about through a wisdom and purpose with which we can fully cooperate and in which we can trust.

Faithfully yours,

Charles Martin

I have a dream today.

I have a dream that one day every valley shall be exalted, every hill and mountain shall be made low, the rough places will be made plains, and the crooked places will be made straight, and the glory of the Lord shall be revealed, and all flesh shall see it together.

Martin Luther King, Jr.

XXV

Death of a President

November 27, 1963

Dear Friends,

I write to you amidst grief and stunned bewilderment. This Sunday afternoon a solemn procession bore our late President to the Capitol rotunda. As I have reflected and sought to bring order to my perplexity, portions of the 139th Psalm have repeatedly been running through my mind.

> —Whither shall I go then from thy spirit? Or whither shall I go then from thy presence?
> —If I climb up into heaven, thou art there; if I go down to hell, thou art there also. . . .
> —If I take the wings of the morning, and remain in the uttermost parts of the sea. . . .
> —Even there also shall thy hand lead me, and thy right hand shall hold me.

It is a strange truth of life that while God is everywhere, always at work and always apparent for them who have eyes to see, He is most apparent as we suffer deeply and know the pain and confusion of hell. It is even so in the hell of these last days.

In His presence, we as a nation know deep shame at the atmosphere that has permitted—even encouraged—the dreadful, violent acts of this weekend. Snide remarks, cheap stories, bitterness and venomous hatred among us—all have played an important part in creating an atmosphere of violence. At St. Albans I have learned firsthand that good men—even great men—who give generously of themselves to our government and deserve our understanding and loyalty, often suffer deeply through the undeserved pain that comes not to them alone but to their families through petty types of harassment, harsh criticism, vengefulness, and unreasoning hatred.

It is also painfully evident that America's easy morality, the disregard for law by individuals and whole communities, the posed cynicism of some of us, the softness of affluence common among many of us—all these have played a part in what has happened. As we view ourselves and our society in the light of President Kennedy's untimely death, "Lord have mercy upon us" is not merely a liturgical phrase; it bears a deep reality to these troubled moments.

If in God's presence our weaknesses as individuals and as a nation are made clear to us, so too are our remarkable courage and nobility. I see great outpourings of sympathy and affection. I hear eloquent tributes. I witness the even more eloquent mute tributes of great masses of people—people moving hurt and bewildered through the streets of Washington, in every part of our nation, in many countries of the world. Such tributes must bring great strength to the bereaved members of Mr. Kennedy's family and to a sorrowing nation.

Both the shame and goodness now known and deeply felt by each of us will affect us in different ways. Those concerned with education must find a new determination so to live that by our teaching and our example we may enable young people to build a world less violent, more ordered, more virtuous, and better than this one. Purged of the cheapness and venom so plainly visible to us now, enobled by the courage and goodness so abundantly poured forth, we can with the Psalmist say:

—Peradventure the darkness shall cover me; then shall my night be turned to day.
—Yea, the darkness is no darkness with thee, but the night is as clear as the day.

May this Thanksgiving be to you and your family a time of thanks for all God's manifold blessings, but especially for the light that has risen out of darkness. Because of that light, may you and all of us be enabled to lead our young people along a better, more noble path.

Faithfully yours,

Charles Martin

Go forth into the world in peace; be of good courage; hold fast to that which is good; render to no one evil for evil; strengthen the faint-hearted; support the weak; help the afflicted; love all persons; serve the Lord; rejoice in the power of the Spirit.

And the blessing of God Almighty, the Father, the Son, and the Holy Ghost, be upon you and remain with you always. Amen.

Liturgical Blessing

XXVI

Good Manners

March 6, 1964

Dear Friends,

A visitor from England chanced to arrive just as the Upper School was leaving the refectory after lunch. As he opened the door of the Lane Johnston Building* to enter, the visitor was engulfed by a stream of boys. He stood aside politely and held the door. Paying scant attention to the stranger, taking for granted that someone was holding the door open for them, the boys thoughtlessly brushed past him. The boys did not mean to be rude; they were merely busy with their own concerns.

Catching sight of me, the visitor attempted to weave his way through the crowded doorway. Twice he was pushed aside. To save further embarrassment, I finally moved among the boys and held them back at the doorway. Looking sheepish, they stopped to let our visitor enter. The visitor maintained courtesy; he said and showed nothing. Containing my discomfiture over the incident, I made pleasant conversation.

*The main building of St. Albans School, which houses the Headmaster's Study.

At lunch the following day, I spoke to our boys about the incident. I told them I knew that no discourtesy had been intended, that they had merely been preoccupied with their own interests. Just the same, I stressed that their behavior had been impolite, speaking at length about manners and about the meaning of courtesy. I felt strongly about what I said, and the boys felt the force of my convictions.

After lunch I went directly to my study to meet with a young friend, a man for whom I have great respect. I found him lost in conversation with a master. The friend was standing with one foot on the arm of my big chair, a chair set apart for parents and friends, a chair on which I do not even allow my dog to sit. Pretending not to notice, I conversed with him while standing; we then sat down and had a good visit. Some time later, the master returned. I commented that I had been troubled by our friend's foot on the chair, asking "Why are so many of Jim's age group so casual in their manners? I am not being critical; I merely want to understand." The master could supply no simple answer. His most helpful observation was that our mutual friend had lived for some time in a region of the country where manners are less formal. There was some truth in what he said, but I was not satisfied. I was still concerned not only about the general lack of respect for things and people but also about the widespread disappearance of thoughtful manners.

I considered the informality and casualness that college living engenders. Some of our colleges and universities furnish examples of overcrowded, unclean living. A casual way of life certainly is not conducive to good manners. Although such conditions do indeed encourage a neglect for basic manners, they are no more to blame than are regions of the country.

I continued the discussion informally at tea time with a group of faculty members. Some of them blamed the home; some blamed society. We mentioned changing standards and the disappearance of absolutes. We even discussed the philosophy of a society that—during the lifetime of most young people—has been at war or is organized to destroy rather than to foster a milieu where people live together with understanding, caring, and sensitivity. Although we did not discuss it, we could have observed that some masters at St. Albans expect and consequently receive courteous behavior in which consideration for others is a norm. Other masters do not receive such courtesy because these amenities are not important to them. Naturally, we arrived at no one solution to the problem.

I finished the day stimulated and determined. I wanted to hammer away persistently, continuously, intelligently, and sensitively to strengthen what to me represents good manners in that part of the world for which I bear responsibility—St. Albans School.

Courteous conduct begins with appearance. If boys have their shoes shined, hair combed, trousers pressed, ties and coats in order, they will feel and act better. We live together formally in the classroom. On the athletic field, we may be informal—but not in school life in general. Neatness and orderliness in dress foster the kind of behavior we wish for in class; slovenliness and informality do not. At St. Albans, therefore, we expect neatness and a degree of easy formality.

To hold a door open or to step aside for another individual shows respect and thoughtfulness, whether the individual be a contemporary or an older person. We all need to be more considerate, more attuned to the feelings of others. Even inanimate objects deserve respect—especially those that belong to someone else.

Do not misunderstand me. I do not expect rigid, robot-like behavior. I realize that the manners and developed formalities of which I write are not ultimates in themselves. I realize, too, that polished manners may hide thoughtless, inconsiderate, even arrogant feelings. Forms are rarely values in themselves; rather, they are vehicles through which goodness can be expressed. Although standards are in a state of flux today, I believe that the manners that have arisen from the civilized living of the past are better vehicles for conveying consideration than are the studied casualness or the self-centeredness of chaotic, unmannered living.

Furthermore, I do recognize that the world has changed. What was considered normal behavior in the day of Queen Victoria is not the rule today. We can at once thank God for the demise of those civilities and also deeply regret their passing.

What we need to develop today is a thoughtful, gracious, considerate way of acting that will enable us to live in mutual harmony and love. This will be more likely to occur if we can preserve and adapt to our times the best of the past. Obviously, neither complete acceptance nor complete rejection of the past will work. Good education proceeds from the known to the unknown.

To believe in good manners and to make them a reality in daily living are two quite different matters. Neither the home nor the school should become a battleground, even to teach what is good. There are limits to what parents and schoolmasters can insist upon without nagging and making life unpleasant for everyone concerned. There are limits even to the power and wisdom of headmasters! Still, if all of us begin holding ourselves to standards of considerate living, looking for examples in those who possess grace, and looking even unto the Throne of Grace, we will slowly grow in graciousness ourselves, communicating that quality not only to our boys but also to others.

Ideally, we should all embrace and share the values and philosophy of a community of people called the Church. Its way of life is sacramental; that is, the Church believes that through the outward and visible is mediated the inward and spiritual. I believe that good manners are, then, visible means of indicating the spiritual—a means that will enable us to live and work together with graciousness, sensitivity, thoughtfulness, and love.

Faithfully yours,

Charles Martin

*Do not look forward in fear to the changes of life; rather look at them with full hope that, as they arise, God, whose very own you are, will deliver you from out of them. He has kept you hitherto, and He will lead you safely through all things, and when you cannot stand it, God will enfold you in his arms. Do not fear what may happen tomorrow; the same everlasting Father who cares for you today will take care of you then and every day. He will either shield you from suffering or will give you unfailing strength to bear it. Be at peace and put aside all anxious thoughts and imaginations.**

St. Francis De Sales (1567-1622)

*Submitted for this book by the late James Henderson, son of "Pop" Henderson, who served St. Albans as chaplain, instructor, and coach from 1918 to 1947.

XXVII

Be Not Anxious for the Morrow

October 15, 1964

Dear Friends,

At a Headmasters' conference in a college in upstate New York, we were served at meals by a group of girls from a high school in a nearby small town. These girls were attractive, natural, and wholesome; they were free of makeup and other marks of sophistication. No boys were about, so we had no opportunity to observe them, but my guess is that we would have found them to be just as natural and wholesome as the girls.

We cannot, of course, reproduce at St. Albans the small-town way of life that made these young people so lovely, but we *can* do something about the practices that force our young people into precocious, unnatural adultlike behavior. We allow, often encourage, and sometimes force boys and girls into sophisticated social patterns for which they are not ready. Dancing classes are begun long before children—boys, at any rate—are ready for them. Dinner parties and dances are arranged when boys would actually prefer to be off doing something more interesting and rewarding to them at their age. Even the parties for youngsters who are ready for mixed social life are usually adult in their pretentions. And this is wrong.

I can understand the pressures of impersonal urban life that can cause mothers to be eager for their daughters to be popular with boys, the pressures of getting children into the "right" social group, the pressures that make parents uncertain about what standards should prevail at parties. Yet we do not have to succumb to these pressures. On the contrary, as parents we have a responsibility to hold to what we believe is right and resist what we believe is wrong. And to me it is wrong to allow—particularly to force—boys into a premature social life. It is right to encourage them to lose themselves in interests and activities natural to boys of their age. Boys need the freedom to grow at their own speed; hence, we parents should strive, as much as possible, to eliminate pressures that force our boys to mature early, to grow at a speed that is not their own.

Such a tendency to push boys ahead of themselves is sometimes noticeable even in the world of schoolboy athletics. One hears, "I'd like Tom to take a sport he can follow in adult life." Such a wish is natural and right only if the boy wants to engage in a certain sport because he is a boy—not solely because he will be able to enjoy it the rest of his life.

Even though sports like basketball, baseball, football, and soccer are often not continued into adult life, boys should have the opportunity and encouragement to enjoy them in the present. On the mantlepiece in my study is a quotation from Justice Holmes that says, "A man should share the action and passion of his times at peril of being judged not to have lived." That statement is as true of a boy's life as it is of an adult's. The sport for a boy to engage in wholeheartedly—packed full and running over—is the one natural to his boyhood, and this is usually a team sport. It is my belief that he will be a better, happier boy and man for having had the experience.

In secondary education there is, unfortunately, the tendency to work doggedly toward some future goal rather than to live fully for today. At St. Albans we seek to be a place where boys grow well, learn, and develop their inborn capacities, where they can live abundantly and without undue anxiety about the future. Living as a boy, going to St. Albans—these are ends in themselves; they need no further justification.

At the beginning of each year, I speak to new parents in the Little Sanctuary. The gist of my annual message is this: "If you are sending your son to St. Albans to get him into Harvard, Yale, or any other college, this is the wrong place to send him. Although attending college is the natural next step in the educational process for boys who attend this School, we are not working toward that end. We are working toward a much more difficult goal, that of getting boys into the Kingdom of Heaven—not a Kingdom far off in the future but the Kingdom of here and now." This may sound like the kind of pious generalization particular to parsons, yet its meaning is clear. Much of life can be made bleak by working for and worrying about some future end. The moment to live is in the present; if today is lived fully and well, then the future will take care of itself. A very respected teacher said: "Be not anxious for the morrow; sufficient unto the day is the evil thereof. Seek ye first the Kingdom of God and all these things shall be added unto you."

A narrow preoccupation with getting into college results in a narrow education. Secondary education can become so narrow that it may neglect the arts or fail to provide an opportunity for development of individual gifts. With the pressures so great to get into the "right" college, it is not surprising that a larger and growing number of students drop out for a year or more to straighten themselves out, to learn not only *where* they are going but also *why*.

Education should be a joy-filled experience. A boy ought to find the same amount of fun in trying to express his feelings in verse or in taking apart and putting together again an automobile engine. Last spring I came over to the School about midnight one night, when all the boys should have been in bed. I noticed a light in a classroom and heard much hilarity within. I stopped at the door to see whether the two Sixth Formers would subside when they saw me. But they never became aware of my presence; they were lost in the fun of solving a mathematical problem. The blackboard was covered with graphs and formulae; slide rules were clicking; discussion was uninhibited. These boys were lost in the joy of discovery, of learning. Even though the hour was late, I left them undisturbed. Education that allows time for a boy to master a skill, conceive an idea, develop an understanding, explore an interest, read broadly, or reflect cannot be had when too much pressure is placed on preparing for the narrow measurements that supposedly assure entrance to a good college.

Unhappily, we headmasters sometimes lose our perspective. At the same meeting where we were served by the unsophisticated young girls, a speaker said, "Schools like ours must prepare for the national need." But schools cannot be custom-made into training centers for national needs, whether the need be for scientists or for any other professional group. We cannot produce, at will, the kinds of scientists this country needs. Good scientists can come only from among the limited number who are endowed by their Creator with the capacity to become good scientists. A gift already present is developed.

The School motto, *Pro Ecclesia et Pro Patria* (For Church and Country), is old-fashioned, but still a worthy educational motto. To put the meaning religiously, the motto denotes an individual's fulfilling in life the purpose for which God created him. It does not mean development of the individual so that he can serve at some time in the future; rather it means growing, learning, sharing, giving, bearing one another's burdens at each moment today and tomorrow.

The Gospel of St. Matthew, Chapter VI, presents a philosophy of life to which I subscribe fully. It includes a profound conviction that man and his affairs are not in man's hands but in the hands of One infinitely more wise and powerful. In terms of education this means that schoolmasters and parents cannot shape any boy or determine his future. They can merely cooperate with Him who does the shaping and planning. Without anxious concern for tomorrow, schoolmasters can go about busily day by day helping boys to live. Parents and schoolmasters who are reasonably humble and wise and who have a reasonable trust in God may enable boys—and themselves as well—to grow into a life that is rich and vital both today and tomorrow.

Faithfully yours,

Charles Martin

O Thou who are wisdom, forever beyond human understanding, yet forever being understood, enable us with minds that are open and humble to learn of Thee in all the common experiences of life and in our relationships with people, but especially in the pain and hurt of man. Then with wisdom born anew in us, may we know the peace that passeth understanding, and may it show forth in our lives to the good of our fellow man. Through Jesus Christ, Amen.

Charles Martin

XXVIII

Blizzard

January 30, 1966

Dear Friends,

We are in the midst of a blizzard. The drifts are high; the wind is strong and biting; the cold is intense. It is good to be home, unless, of course, one should be somewhere else.

Early this morning it was black, cold, and forbidding. I was loath to get moving, but after shoveling out the snow that had blown in the house when I opened the door and after shoveling a path to the street, I felt better. It was exhilarating to pit myself against the wind and snow. At School and later at the Cathedral, I felt positively comfortable, even self-righteous. The latter state was quickly dispelled by a brief conversation I had with a young acolyte:

"Hello. How did you get here?"

"Walked and hitchhiked."

"Where do you live?"

"Out by the District line."

Back home, I reflected upon the day, making a few observations evoked by the blizzard. It was rough when I first went out into the storm, but it was not nearly as rough as I had anticipated. It has been my experience that most of our problems are in our minds, not in the facts of life themselves. Twenty-five miles may seem a considerable distance to an Easterner; one-hundred miles, a modest one to a Westerner. Mental states and attitudes can make a great difference. One fears to face up to a long pull, a difficult situation. When he does, however, he finds the pull not so long, the situation not so difficult as he had anticipated. No matter how long the pull or how great the difficulty, one often discovers that the experience has been strengthening—at times even exhilarating.

On my way to church this morning, I saw my neighbor, the choirmaster at a Silver Spring church, cleaning off his car with a broom. Beside him was a shovel, and his car was parked downhill. My guess is that having made this kind of preparation and having gotten such an early start, he will be playing the organ in his church, and he will be there on time. One does not meet life successfully unless he is prepared. And most of us make few preparations either for storms of the atmosphere or for storms of life.

Only a few persons were present at the Cathedral this morning, but, to me, the service had a greater relevance than usual. We gave thanks for the difficult and demanding in life that make for strength, for the new appreciation of our dependence one upon another. We remembered those made to suffer by the storm and by all the hardships of life. Even the Collect for the Day held a new meaning:

> O God, who knowest us to be set in the midst of so many and great dangers, that by reason of the frailty of our nature we cannot always stand upright; Grant to us such strength and protection as may support us in all dangers and carry us through all temptations; through Jesus Christ our Lord. Amen.

When one faces life as it comes, not evading the difficult, he becomes stronger; he learns a new sense of dependence; he is granted an inner peace and sense of well-being that enable him better to face life.

Now back to my acolyte. If I had been his parent, I would have been greatly troubled at the thought of his going out on such a hazardous trip; it would not have been easy to allow him to do it. Yet, I am sure their boy is stronger and better for this experience. Life has risks. Risks must be faced, not avoided. It is amazing the strengths we discover within us when we are really tested. We can scale a fourteen-foot fence when the bull is after us; we can pass a difficult algebra course when we make up our minds to; we can face sad and tragic losses when we must and, in the process, become finer human beings.

American life today does not make these truths at once evident. Our whole emphasis is upon making life easier and more comfortable. The escalator saves us from walking up a flight of stairs; a push-button gadget saves us from getting up to turn on the TV. The thermostat saves us from firing the furnace and the air conditioner from fanning ourselves. On the whole, comforts are not bad in themselves, and we ought to accept and enjoy them. On the other hand, we ought not to be softened and misled by comforts. There will always be flights of stairs to be climbed. Our hearts, minds, and bodies need to be ready for them. Intellectual effort will always be required; we ought not to allow our minds to become flabby. While temperatures can be manipulated within our homes, the rise and fall of events in life cannot be controlled. We need to be able to meet and adjust to them.

When I finish this letter, I will call upon two young friends whose fathers have just died. Death is the ultimate reality we have to meet. We generally ignore death and seek to escape its reality with all kinds of euphemisms and strange customs, but we cannot escape its finality. Ultimately, we all must meet it.

There are hosts of other less painful, but still demanding, experiences we are called upon to meet in life. We must be prepared to meet these storms as they occur. As we face them we shall be surprised and pleased at the understanding and kindness that are gifts from others and from God. It is heartening to learn that we have resources outside ourselves; it is beneficial to depend upon others.

Storms are a part of life — a good part. It can be exhilarating to be in their midst.

Faithfully yours,

Charles Martin

O God, lift us by the might of Thy presence that we may be still and know that Thou art God. Quiet us, refresh and renew us, and grant that Thy Holy Spirit may in all things direct and rule our hearts. Through Jesus Christ our Lord. Amen.

Adapted by Charles Martin

XXIX

Lenten Reflections

February 10, 1966

Dear Friends,

At a weekly breakfast meeting of alumni responsible for planning one of our School's programs, a young lawyer commented to me, "I had a touch of grippe yesterday, so I stayed home. I had taken some work home with me, and do you know that I accomplished more in a half day at home than I could have done in a whole day at the office. It was a pleasure to be free from all the interruptions that come at the office." We discussed how necessary it is to get away from things, not only to accomplish tasks, but also to get a longer view and a better perspective. His final comment was, "The trouble is that we have to get sick or something worse before we stop and take stock of ourselves and the direction of our lives."

I wanted to sum up our conversation a different way by saying, "You hard-working, generous young man, what you are talking about is the purpose of Lent." However, I thought the comment might sound too preachy, so it went unsaid. Yet I don't mind being preachy occasionally in one of these letters. I offer you, then, some reflections on the meaning of Lent.

When I arrived at School this morning, instead of rushing to my desk as I usually do — intent on getting to the day's work — I stopped to chat with one of our custodians who was straightening up the Common Room. This man has had all the troubles of Job and a few more. These troubles have left their mark on him, but not in the way one would expect. Instead of resulting in hurt and bitterness, they have given him a quality of dignity and inner peace few of us possess. Like Job, he has emerged victorious from his problems, having gained a sturdy trust in life's ultimate goodness. I felt better for having spoken to him.

At breakfast I joined the boys. On one side of me was an exuberant young man, barely able to control his high spirits. On the other side sat a boy whose pert, lively spirit was only occasionally revealed in a bright smile or in a shy but illuminating comment. Next to him sat an athletically built boy who seemed to carry the weight of the world on his shoulders — and so on around the table. Each boy, in his own way, was a pleasure to be with, and I benefited from their company.

My regular practice in the morning is to hurry to my study, conscious of letters to write, persons to see, decisions to make, reports to finish, telephone calls to answer. Today, though, I had varied my usual schedule by taking time out to do what I most enjoy — be with people. It is in people and with people that God's wisdom and goodness are revealed.

After breakfast that morning, I tried to pray for the sick and troubled in the School family. Prayer does not come easily to me; it is hard work. I cannot merely say words or read prayers. I try to place myself in God's presence, give thanks, and then — one by one — hold in God's presence those for whom I would pray. Today I finished praying with clearer understanding and a sense of inner peace.

A few days ago I prepared a schedule of Lenten services and meetings that would accompany this letter. Realizing that the schedule was sizable, I consulted with parents, alumni, and faculty members about it. All we succeeded in doing, however, was adding another service to the list! A discerning master remarked to me, "You are going to be so busy in Lent that you will not be able to practice what you preach." It may be so! And I am not unmindful of the irony of increasing our scheduled activities, for Lent is a time set aside in the Christian calendar for us to simplify life, to drop some of the busyness so characteristic of our lives.

For me, however, being with people in the spirit of the Teacher whom I would serve brings meaning and order to my life as well as a sense of usefulness and joy that is peace.

Lent is traditionally meant to be a time when, together with members of the Christian family, we are enabled to lay aside our troubles and anxieties. Ideally, we are then able to face the future with new openness, relaxed purposefulness, and an eagerness to learn and to grow. With renewed energy and a fresh perspective, we are then able to see and to accept the good and the true. We need to take time to be with our family, our friends, and our God, to rid ourselves of some of our activities.

I know that ridding ourselves of trivialities and getting down to relationships is not easy and takes some doing. A few months ago I had a wonderful experience of what it means to be free of interruptions. The telephone wires were severed by excavation near the Cathedral, and for a day or so we had no incoming or outgoing calls. I have never enjoyed such quiet since I have been at St. Albans, nor have I gotten so much done! As far as I could observe, no one missed all the talking and activity that would otherwise have ensued. I realize that much of the activity of my life could be eliminated, with much gain to all concerned. But how this is to be effected must be determined by each one of us. I cannot presume to suggest how you could go about it even if I knew.

In another age — not too long ago — I would have made the following pronouncements: "Make a rule for Lent, say your prayers and attend church; fast and give up something; make a special offering; remember the Lord thy God." Lent and its practices may seem, in these days, to belong to a bygone era, yet many of the practices and purposes of Lent I have mentioned still pertain. Yesterday or today, however, the central meaning of Lent is the same: " . . . they that wait upon the Lord shall renew their strength; they shall mount up with wings as eagles; they shall run, and not be weary, and they shall walk, and not faint."

Faithfully yours,

Charles Martin

. . . . What can we do? We can stand firm against pressures we know are wrong. We can create pressures of our own, good ones. We can quit trying to keep up with the Joneses. We can dare to say "no." We can come to grips with the changing times in which we live. In our youth . . . young people were less mobile; they were less hostile, restless, and rebellious; there were more checks and balances; there was more authority. We can't turn the clock back; we are where we find ourselves. We have to grapple with things as they are. But we can. We worship a God who cares, who supports the right, who holds up the arms of those who do the right.

We've been asleep.

*The Rev. Robert Nelson Back**

*Paraphrase from part of a sermon by the Reverend Robert Nelson Back, then Rector of St. Luke's, Darien, Connecticut (January 29, 1965).

XXX

In the Midst of Dramatic Change

May 17, 1967

Dear Friends,

Recently I received a letter from a young man who teaches in a coeducational school in one of the Western states. Part of the letter follows:

> . . . . From our small school seven have already been expelled: two for having sexual intercourse, three for drinking in the dormitory, and two for smoking marijuana . . . . I take these unhappy cases as evidence of the turbulence of the times . . . . I am enough of a pessimist to suspect that the spirit of Berkeley and of the 'swinging world' will come to the East; it shouldn't surprise me if before long it comes to St. Albans . . . .

Yesterday a friend came to see me about his daughter, a casualty of the "swinging" life on a great university campus. Able, sensitive, and highly idealistic, she had, as a high-school girl, been quite conventional, but she quickly became "far out" once in college. Adopting the dress, uncleanliness, and manners of an extreme group, she became a militant agitator for a multitude of causes. As a consequence, her studies suffered, and she had been dropped from college. Her father was understandably distraught.

What could I do? I could listen and express my sympathy for and understanding of his and his daughter's distress. I could appreciate how an intelligent, sensitive girl (who had inherited some of her father's stubbornness and rebelliousness) might be deeply troubled by the state of a world she had no part in creating. I suggested that time, the innate goodness of the girl, and the sensitivity and good judgment of the family would bring some balance and health to this disturbing situation.

Having reflected upon both the letter and the conversation, I naturally thought about our boys. My immediate reaction: these are extremes; I don't see such behavior among our boys. And I don't. Occasionally an alumnus returns from college who is — in both dress and manners — the male counterpart of my friend's daughter. To myself, I explain the boy in terms of problems I know were already within him when he was with us. At St. Albans our boys continue to be reasonably uncontaminated by the vagaries of the "far out" world. We are yet to be troubled by the events described in the young master's letter or experienced by my friend's daughter.

But does this belief, so easy and natural to a headmaster, stand up under scrutiny? How little does a headmaster know! Only the best front is presented before him. He sees neatness and polite behavior. To see behind appearances, a headmaster needs imagination, discernment, an ear close to the ground, and an acquaintanceship with the world as it is. If he has these qualities, a headmaster may then discover that his boys are merely experiencing problems common to their peer group. No young person is completely isolated from his culture. Based on the distinctiveness of his background and his personality, each young person experiences the pressures of the times in which he lives.

As we are all aware, we are living in the midst of dramatic change. Values once taken for granted appear to have vanished. Uncertainty about right and wrong has replaced certainty. The structures and supports of the past appear to have crumbled. As life becomes increasingly complex, answers are not at once obvious. Now we see through a glass darkly. How shall we get out of Vietnam? How shall we build the Great Society? How shall we meet the many crises of growing up?

While some among us can make black and white judgments, most cannot. If we as adults encounter difficulty making absolute judgments, how much more difficulty must young persons encounter. To live wisely we all need guidance; however, young persons need it more than most. Yet, sadly, many of us — parents and schoolmasters — find it hard to render help because our young people turn a deaf ear, choosing not to accept our advice.

Recent experiences have made this dilemma very clear. Just before vacation, I spoke to School leaders about their responsibilities, particularly in regard to drinking. I was in good form, and I was saying exactly what I meant. However, I soon realized that I was not reaching the boys. A very obvious curtain had dropped between me and them. Boy after boy stopped listening; mind after mind turned off, moving to its own concern. Realizing my message was not being communicated, I quickly concluded my talk. The boys, having heard the same message before, realized that it did not speak to their problems.

A few minutes after the meeting broke up, two of the boys came to see me. As we visited, I was gradually clued in. The scales dropped from my eyes as I learned about the true nature of the boys' social life. And, indeed, it did not have much to do with what I had been discussing. Although the boys had known it, I had not. I simply had not realized how common drinking was among our students, how much the use of alcohol was taken for granted, how different from mine were their standards of behavior and of right and wrong. They had heard my message repeatedly from adults, and — since they lived in another world — they had long since stopped paying attention.

At our opening faculty meeting last fall, a gracious lady — a widely experienced doctor — spoke to us about the sex practices of young people she met in her work. She did not speak in sterile medical language; she did not use the polite euphemisms of ordinary conversation. She spoke in the language of the streets. The effect was shattering. Whether I was jarred by hearing this lovely lady use gutter language or whether I needed to be "shook up," I just don't know. I do know, however, that listening to her enabled me to understand that my values about sex — my fixed moral values — prevented me from communicating with young people. My values, based upon traditional Christian thinking, had always held. Even if I or anyone else departed from them, they still stood. Now I saw what I vaguely had known but had not allowed to sink in: young people do not necessarily accept or live by these values. Rather, they are seeking, but not yet finding, a new set of values. Recognizing this, not only could I better understand young people's problems, but I also felt I could communicate with them better.

Barriers to understanding between youth and age are not related to years but rather to beliefs, values, prejudices, and the inability to see and hear clearly. One of our masters — well along in years — speaks and listens to even the youngest students with a quality of sympathy and understanding that engenders their love and respect.

Does all this mean that adults must put aside their beliefs, their standards in order to communicate with boys? No. It *does* mean that adults must recognize there are other sets of values to be sympathetically understood, not condemned. If understanding between generations exists, abiding beliefs will speak with great force to young persons — in fact, to persons of any age.

Let us not be misled into thinking that, amidst the confusions of today, young people are a weaker or poorer lot than those of another day. Such is not the case. About a year ago, a young grandchild of mine was killed in an accident. Among the kind, helpful letters I received was one from a sixteen-year-old girl.

> I have something sadly wonderful to share with you. Please know that God has worked through the loss of your grandson. When I heard the news, I cried. This is the first time I have cried since reacting to the shock of my father's death four years ago. Can you imagine my joy at finally breaking through a wall of stoicism to feel life. I had been pretending that pain was a part of life that did not exist.

This was a remarkable letter from a person so young. Though young people may appear more troubled today, less sure of right and wrong, seemingly less responsible, I believe they are just as fine as those of any other generation. But they will listen and learn only if we understand them and their different beliefs. Discarding past standards that are transient and ephemeral, we must communicate to them the eternal and everlasting values.

A poet ages ago did this for his generation. Since he was speaking of the Eternal One, he was expressing values that are as meaningful to us today as they were for his generation and countless generations since. I said that poem, the Twenty-third Psalm, at a sickbed just a few hours ago.

> The Lord is my shepherd, I shall not want . . . Yea, though I walk through the valley of the shadow of death, I will fear no evil: for thou *art* with me. . . . Surely goodness and mercy shall follow me all the days of my life; and I will dwell in the house of the Lord forever.

From the experience of his time, this poet — who dwelt among a nomadic people — arrived at fundamental understandings about life. God was seen as a shepherd who guarded, protected, searched out, comforted, healed, and lived forever with His people. For centuries, this truth has strengthened those able to glimpse the truths that lie behind the poet's pastoral imagery. It is for us today — living in far different times and circumstances — to express the abiding values that give meaning to our lives. Even though we may not be able to do so in words, we *can* express these values through our lives; we shall thus speak with compelling force.

With our children, we must hold to standards we believe to be right, not with softness, but with the firmness of love. God working through us can shape people who walk in the ways of righteousness — even in the midst of dramatic change.

Faithfully yours,

Charles Martin

Disturb us, Lord, when we are too well pleased with ourselves, when our dreams have come true because we have dreamed too little, when we arrived safely because we sailed too close to shore. Disturb us, Lord, when with the abundance of the things we possess, we have lost our thirst for the water of life.

Stir us, Lord, to dare more boldly, to venture on wider seas, where storms will show your mastery; where losing sight of land, we shall find the stars. We ask you to push back the horizons of our hopes and to push us into the future in strength, courage, hope, and love. Amen.

Bob Darwall, Former Chaplain
Cranbrook School
*Bloomfield Hills, Michigan**

---

*Submitted for the book by the Rev. Roger Bowen.

XXXI

Unrest and Protest

July 1, 1968

Dear Friends,

The recent convulsions at Columbia University have implications for all education — even for us at St. Albans. This letter considers those implications. While the occurrences at Columbia grew out of that institution's own life and are distinctive to it, the unrest that brought its students and a substantial part of its faculty into rebellion and caused a complete collapse of the University exists not only at a nationwide level but also at a worldwide level. No college or university is immune from the restless forces stirring among us.

The causes of student unrest are complex and deeply rooted in today's society. Though these causes may never be fully understood, certain facts are clear. In almost every college and university of any size there is a small group of revolutionaries — Students for a Democratic Society (SDS) — dedicated to the overthrow of the established order in educational institutions and in American life. This militant group foments disorder, exploiting campus unrest and institutional weakness.

But even without any stimulation from activist political groups, students are restless, not only because they share the prevailing unrest of the times, but also because they are young and idealistic, less willing to compromise, more sensitive to change. Values that have given support and meaning to the lives of their elders are brushed aside as being irrelevant and hypocritical. Most unfortunately, the law has lost much of its authority under the impact of civil disobedience and moral imperatives.

Furthermore, students have their own distinctive causes for unrest. With some justification, they often feel they are mere numbers in a huge institution. Their courses frequently appear to be unrelated to their experience. They often see in their education and in the institution of which they are a part no moral dimension whatever. Harold Taylor, former president of Sarah Lawrence, put it this way:

> The universities have become corporations for producing, transmitting, and marketing knowledge, and in doing so have lost their intellectual and moral identity. At the time they should have been creative centers for the development of strategies for peace, disarmament, and world unity, they were busy with Defense Department contracts . . . . It is no wonder that a new generation of students . . . . conscious of the visible flaws in their society and its educational system, has risen to challenge the aimlessness and the intellectual lethargy of the big university in America.

St. Albans School in not likely to undergo a seizure by students or to exhibit any violent evidence of unrest today or tomorrow. Still, St. Albans is in the world and will thus experience, to varying degrees, contemporary problems. It is for us at St. Albans to recognize that fact and to seek to give our students an education ever more useful, meaningful, and relevant to our changing times. Let me outline some of the directions in which we have been moving.

Our students do not suffer, as do students in large universities, from being mere faceless numbers. Relations in the classroom, on the athletic field, and in our common life are close. Still, we are occasionally shocked to realize that we know only the surface boy, not the real boy. And we tend to understand students in terms of our experiences and not theirs, oblivious that the world of young people today and the world of our youth are poles apart.

Conscious of this polarity, last fall we arranged to hold three long weekend conferences. Attended by prefects, members of the School vestry, and a group of masters, the first two meetings focused upon examining School life and seeking ways to strengthen it. A third conference, attended by twenty boys representing all the forms and by six masters, dealt with a group of actual case studies of schoolboy problems, written up and considered according to the Case Study Method made popular by the Harvard Business School. Boys looked at problems from the viewpoint of faculty members and parents; masters looked at problems from the boy's viewpoint. Out of all this came a degree of mutual understanding greater than we had known before. A Sixth Former gave the ultimate accolade to the faculty when he commented, "Sir, I think there is a greater 'gap' between the Sixth Form* and the Third Form** than between the faculty and the Sixth Form. From these conferences came proposals for changes in student government that will give students more responsibilities in the School's day-to-day functioning.

In the same spirit of searching, a substantial part of our faculty has met biweekly during the year to make an exhaustive study of our curriculum. While the work of the committee is far from complete, change is in the air. Old courses are being reexamined; new courses are being introduced; new relations are being established with nearby schools and with the community at large. For example, we have instituted a course in computers and programming and will offer two new film courses.

Equally important have been the increased number of community leaders who have shared in our School life and the increased number of students and faculty members who have shared in the general life of the community. Perhaps the most significant effort we have made toward community involvement has

---

*Sixth Form — twelfth grade at St. Albans.
**Third Form — ninth grade at St. Albans.

been our Senior Project. For two weeks at the end of winter term, all our seniors went off for new educational experiences in government and community agencies, businesses, and industry.

The group of boys who worked in hospitals had the most rewarding experiences, largely because they were dealing directly with people. These students sat in on staff discussions, viewed operations, and generally became involved in the daily work of the hospital. One mother wrote, "This was the greatest educational experience my son has had in his lifetime." Likewise, one of the boys who worked in a Congressman's office commented, "I learned more about life and the U.S. Government in two weeks than I had learned all year in school."

In a further effort to effect meaningful changes, we will be studying our chapel services and our Sacred Studies course. In the midst of the world's turbulence, it is constantly more evident that we must help our boys to hold fast to abiding values, if we are to set forth a way of life that offers support and an authority that instills confidence. Our graduates are going to attend the Columbias of our country; these institutions may be as revolutionary tomorrow as they are today. Our boys will need values to believe in, respect for and faith in authority, and confidence in themselves and in their abilities to bring about meaningful change. In this era of student unrest, it is good for us to remember that young revolutionary, Jesus Christ, Our Lord, who was dedicated to an absolute authority, God, whom he called Father.

Faithfully yours,

Charles Martin

God, our Father, as your Word became man for our salvation, grant that our many words — both those we read and those we write and speak — may make your presence known and work to our good, both in this world and the next. This we ask through your Son, the Word of Life. Amen.

*Paul Piazza**

---

*Paul Piazza is chairman of the St. Albans English Department.

XXXII

Of Christmas Cards and Books

December 31, 1968

Dear Friends,

It is New Year's weekend. Resolutely, I am staying away from School — just puttering around, watching football games, thumbing through books, savoring Christmas cards. At the moment, I am reflecting upon the meaning of Christmas cards.

I love to receive Christmas cards, even though I don't exclaim over them or decorate a room with them. I look at the cards as they arrive, fidget with them a bit, and put them aside until I have more leisure in which to enjoy them. Leisure, however, simply does not come. Christmas cards do not merely evoke memories; they also represent persons, with all their goodness, their strange and curious humanity. Through these greetings, which bring together past, present, and future, I come to learn something of the wonder and mystery of life.

One card came from a young alumnus in the military service, bearing a long note about his visits in Europe. The lad has had some problems, but I could tell from the feel of his words that he is beginning to solve them. Another card perplexes me. It comes from someone with whom I thought I had only a casual association. Apparently, in some way unrealized by me, I had touched his life, for he wrote a very moving greeting. Through such messages, one realizes anew the mystery of human communication and human relationships. A cheerful, brightly colored greeting from the small son of a neighbor caused me to know again that there is nothing lovelier than a little boy — unless, of course, it is a little girl. From the past and present arrive card after card bearing persons and experiences — and life is richer and better for their coming.

The selection of a Christmas card is, for me, no simple matter. Instead of choosing a card from the multitude available, I try to develop and send out a greeting that speaks of the life and convictions of the School. This year's card, which pictures the Peace Cross over Washington (as depicted on a needlepoint kneeler in our chapel) and bears a quotation from Judge Learned Hand, brought a greater response than usual. Many expressed appreciation for the Judge's eloquent description of the spirit of liberty; many troubled about Vietnam commented on the Peace Cross, expressing their hope for a world free from war.

While it is no longer possible for me to sign and write a note on each card I send, I do remember and think of each individual before I put a card in its envelope. I have time to wonder about a new baby of an alumnus and his wife, to ask for some information about a graduate, or to express appreciation to a colleague. To me, sending a card is an act of prayer.

* * * * * *

And, now, if you will permit me a marked shift in subject matter — from Christmas cards to a Christmas gift. I had originally intended to end this letter with an expression of appreciation for your thoughtfulness and good will to St. Albans School and an earnest wish for a Happy New Year. Then I got up to stretch before writing the final paragraph, wandered over to the tree, and picked up *The Lawrenceville Stories* by Owen Johnson, a Christmas gift from a close friend and colleague. Leafing through it started a train of thoughts and reminiscences that I would like to share with you.

For those of you too young to remember, *The Lawrenceville Stories* are wonderful schoolboy tales that titillated those of us who lived in that innocent age just prior to World War I. The very sight of the dust jacket, which pictures characters from the book, evoked a flood of nostalgic memories. Yet I am hesitant about reading this book because of disappointing excursions into rereading books affectionately remembered from my past.

Last summer I collected a half dozen of what I remembered to be great Western novels by Zane Grey. I looked forward to a couple of days of escape into the pleasure of my boyhood. But when I got around to the actual reading, I was shattered and disillusioned. *Riders of the Purple Sage,* which I had eagerly begun with near reverence, was so filled with purple prose, so flat that I could not finish it. Almost in a kind of defense against the past, I bundled the whole Zane Grey collection under my arm, rushed to the library, dumped the load, and ran. The same disenchantment proved to be true when I settled down to reread other boyhood favorites. These classics — *The Deerslayer, Ivanhoe, Jane Eyre* — simply didn't read well to me today. Thus I will move hesitantly into *The Lawrenceville Stories.*

It is pleasant to look back to a past when boys were just boys and their major preoccupations were outwitting their natural enemies (the masters) or engaging in pranks with an element of high risk but inevitable good humor and fun. These were boys whose school careers ended with a glorious football victory or with a girl by the hand, walking romantically into the future. That kind of idyll makes the life of today's schoolboy, as pictured by Knowles in *A Separate Peace* or by Salinger in *Catcher in the Rye,* seem like a horrible nightmare.

But neither the idyllic school days of Owen Johnson nor the stark, neurotic school days of modern writers represent the truth. When one searches his memory and recalls the pain of shyness, the hurt of slights, the self-doubts, the frustrations, the sense of guilt — then reality forces its way through nostalgia and the glow of memory dims or disappears. On the whole, I believe that the schoolboy of today is a healthier, better person because his abilities are more fully developed than in the past and his individual interests are given such wide opportunities for expression.

Yet when such advantages are recognized, one can yet wish for a more simple, relaxed atmosphere. Our present search for academic excellence often leads us to ignore human development. The pressures of tests and of getting into college promote not health, not even academic excellence, but uneven development, anxiety, and — sometimes — neuroses, with confused or nonexistent values being the byproduct.

While in a simpler day the job at St. Albans was to teach religious truth and maintain a Christian spirit in the School, today our job is that and much more. The responsibility and opportunity of St. Albans, independent of community and state, free from passing fads and fashions, is to hold to some values of the past, to search restlessly for truth in the present, and to maintain a community in which a student can develop his own distinctive individuality. To put it another way, our task is to raise up men whole and fit, free of anxieties and neuroses, able to meet the complex, frustrating demands of today and tomorrow.

All of which brings me back to Christmas cards and their message. May the good will, the generous thoughtfulness, the good cheer, the new and good life that is so fully among us at Christmas be with you this year. Happy New Year.

Faithfully yours,

Charles Martin

We are in the midst of the most radical revolution in the history of mankind. This revolution is a transformation of the human environment and of man himself by technological progress which, beginning about two centuries ago, has now acquired enormous momentum. It is changing the way men live, not only their work and their houses, their food and their communications and their pleasures, but it is changing also the structure of the human family and the chemistry of the human personality.

Walter Lippman

XXXIII

Reflections: Student Disorders

March 5, 1969

Dear Friends,

Less than a year ago, I wrote a letter regarding student unrest in universities. Since then, it appears that the state of affairs has escalated to frightening proportions. None of us would deny that we are living in the middle of a revolution. Though it may seem to embattled educators that all students at all schools are erupting in picket lines, mass demonstrations, sleep-ins, confrontations, and various forms of violence, happily such is not the case. Most students go on — or wish to go on — with their studies as usual. However, even these students are profoundly affected by the activists and by the times. Thus, they know a deep measure of unrest. It is with these students that we are largely concerned.

For ease of consideration — and perhaps too tidily — I will divide my students into three groups, using terminology that verges on jargon: the alienated and uncommitted, the partly alienated and uncommitted, and the alienated but committed.

The first group may be exemplified by a boy we shall call Paul. After Paul attended a year of school in the West, we welcomed him back. He had been a gifted writer, a talented artist, and a promising athlete. In short, he had been a positive influence in School life. But when he returned, we knew he had changed. The latent uneasiness that we had earlier known in him had increased markedly. Paul dropped out of athletics and could not bring himself to paint or to write. His friendships were few, confined to those who, like himself, were troubled. Regretfully, we were forced to decide that he would have to leave School. Now, at home, he is receiving medical care that will enable him to live in today's world.

If this were one boy, we would not be overly concerned. But there are many other able, fine boys like him who walk to the beat of a different drummer. Alienated and uncommitted, they drop out of school and college for mental institutions or go off into hippiedom or simply become the flotsam and jetsam of society.

A much larger group of young people are those who are troubled somewhat like Paul but who are still able to carry on in the normal world. These I choose to call the partly-alienated and uncommitted. I think of a boy, now in college, with whom I spent much time last year. He is interested in films, in roaring sounds that adults do not recognize as music, in avant-garde art forms, in friends his parents feel are undesirable — but he is not interested in school. I remember how he patiently explained to me that his parents wanted him to go to deb parties, to make friends with the proper people because they would be useful to him in the future. He did not find that a valid motive; further, those who were his friends (unlike those his parents wished him to know) had values he appreciated — compassion, understanding, and love. A number of boys like him have dropped out of college after a few months. Their courses were not interesting, and they wanted to do something worthwhile. Some have joined Vista, the Peace Corps, or the International Volunteer Corps in Vietnam. Others of this group have remained physically in college but reside emotionally and mentally in their own worlds of eclectic interests. This group of boys is searching, but they have not yet found a commitment in life.

Then there are the alienated but wholly committed. George

is a good example. A fine student, athlete, and leader, he showed deep concern for the world but few signs of being alienated. Unsure about college, George decided he could not take part in the Vietnam War. Instead, he joined the Peace Corps in Latin America. Though he enjoyed his work, he was troubled. I have not seen George, but his friends tell me that he has become a member of Students for a Democratic Society. Two years in the Peace Corps, worsening race relations, and the deepening tragedy of Vietnam seem to have convinced him that the present structure of our government cannot meet the needs of our people. Now back at university, George is deeply committed to bringing about change, peacefully if possible, violently if necessary.

What can one do about these disorders among young people? What should one's attitude be? I know what mine frequently is. When we have a homecoming for our alumni in college, the beards, long and tangled hair, and strange-looking persons whom I have trouble recognizing from two or three years before make me want to shrink into the distant past, muttering, "Martin, what have you done? What has your life been worth?" Conversations with university officials who have wrestled with student violence and, above all, lurid pictures and reports on TV and in the press of student excesses and faculty faults make me grind my teeth and say to myself that what is needed is force. My background tells me that these young people need parents who will use an occasional heavy foot. Better yet, these boys need a stint in the Marine Corps.

These are my reactions until I realize that however much we need firmness at school and earnestness at home, these qualities by themselves are not enough. The present generation gap is unlike any in the past — wider, deeper, even different in kind. It can be bridged only if to firmness and earnestness we bring flexibility and a stretching of the mind and imagination. To do so is extraordinarily difficult for anyone, particularly for those of us who are older or who do not come in contact with youth.

A man named Marshall McLuhan, by stretching my mind and imagination, has given me greater insights into the problems of education and of young people than has any other author I have read in a decade. He has helped me to understand that the school, the home, and the church are no longer the only — or even the primary — educational influences on youth. These influences have been superseded by other means of education — TV, radio, films, the theater, magazines, newspapers — in fact, by all the media of the modern world.

It is no longer true that old and young are exposed to the same influences. How many of us can quote the lyrics of a Beatles' song? How many have seen "The Graduate" or "Hair"? How many have read a student underground newspaper or the publications of the Grove Press? If we have, we have screened them by a set of values that young people do not possess. The values that the older generation possesses belong to a different culture than that of today. Our values are not their values; our world is not their world.

In such a world, formal education naturally seems dull and unchallenging. Physically present in the classroom, these students dwell elsewhere. With the richness of life enveloping them through films, radio, TV, and the other media, they are bored with ordered bits of book knowledge in the classroom. They want to learn about life, from life. When this is not understood and adjustments are not made, some students doggedly plod ahead, learning in school with their left hand and learning in life with their right. Others drop out; still others rebel.

One cannot condone violence by students, nor can one excuse students from personal responsibility for their aberrant forms of behavior, but neither can one excuse an educational institution from supine indifference to change, nor huge universities from massive impersonality, nor institutions from failing to respond to human needs. To read the Cox Report on the convulsions at Columbia is to recognize that changes in administration and structure have been long overdue there and at many similar institutions. When I spoke with one of our troubled alumni currently doing graduate work at a great state university, I felt the need for sweeping changes. "When I registered," said the alumnus, "I was given a number. In a lecture course with more than one thousand students, I was not a person, not even a name, but a number. Exams were marked not by a professor but by an IBM machine; when my grade appeared on a bulletin board, it appeared under my number. Maybe the course was an educational experience for my number and for the computer, but not for me."

The revolution we are now experiencing is a time full of pain, but it is also a time full of hope. The ability of our educational institutions to adjust — *our* ability to adjust — to the changes brought about by the revolution will determine in large measure how our students adjust. And in them is our hope. If we are able to hold fast to that which is abiding and good and to slough off the transient, then our young people will know less hurt; consequently, the hope that is in them will be more quickly fulfilled. If, with the understanding and wisdom that age and maturity are supposed to bring, we are able to stand by, listen to, guide, and support the troubled and alienated, then there is hope that out of the travail of the present will be born a new world, a better one than we have known.

Faithfully yours,

Charles Martin

. . . whatsoever things are true, whatsoever things are honest, whatsoever things are just, whatsoever things are pure, whatsoever things are lovely, whatsoever things are of good report; if there be any virtue, if there be any praise, think on these things.

Philippians 4:8

XXXIV

The Drug Problem

December 16, 1969

Dear Friends,

At a recent parent meeting, a mother remarked, "It's so good to hear your view on drugs. I've been very worried about Jimmy." Smilingly I reassured her, "I wouldn't be concerned about Jimmy." "But I am," she continued. "This whole business is just very upsetting, and one doesn't know what will happen these days." Although I tried to reassure her, I could certainly understand her concern. Drugs are a recent phenomenon, and we don't yet know what to make of them.

Three or four years ago, it would have been unthinkable for me to be writing a parent letter on this subject. Drugs were then associated with a fringe element of society, an element about whom we knew little and with whom we had no relation. The suddenness with which the drug problem has burst upon the world is both startling and unsettling. An alumnus told me that he had graduated from Princeton in 1965 without ever having heard of a student's using drugs. Yet when he returned to Princeton a year later, he found their use quite common. We now know that marijuana has been experimented with or used by a majority of university students. While the number of students in high school who use marijuana may not be as large, its use still represents a legitimate cause for concern.

It is unrealistic for us to believe that St. Albans can be isolated and protected from the world or that our students will have experiences that differ from those of their contemporaries. There might have been a day when a school or a family could hold to its own standards and ignore those of others, but if there was such a day, it does not now exist. Through TV, radio, newspapers, and motion pictures, young people at St. Albans will naturally share the thoughts, experiences, and values of society in general. I don't mean to imply that we can do nothing about the values of our young people. Indeed, we can and we must.

At the outset, I would like to differentiate between two groups of drugs. Marijuana ("pot") is very widely used; however, we do not yet know its addictive potential or the effects of long-term usage. The so-called "hard" drugs — amphetamines, LSD, and heroin — are of greater concern to the community at large. In my judgment, our boys have thus far avoided hard drugs. A few troubled boys among us may experiment with the latter group, but I believe they represent a minority. Their problems need consideration beyond the scope of this letter.

Although the hard facts about the nature and effects of marijuana have yet to be determined by the medical profession, my own attitude toward the use of pot is unambiguous. The use of pot is wrong. It is wrong because it is illegal; because we do not yet know how damaging it can be; because those who use it are more apt to go on to hard drugs than those who do not use it; and because it deals with and supports a criminal element of society.

These attitudes differ markedly from those held by the average young person. He argues that while at the moment pot is illegal, the laws that govern it are absurd and are being changed in some states. To this I agree. Some of the laws about pot are being changed. But the fact remains that the drug is illegal. As for harm, the student argues that he can say (from experience) that the drug has few or no ill effects, compared with those of tobacco or alcohol. Here there is doubt, for we all know that tobacco and alcohol are harmful. We also know that pot is harmful and potentially addictive, but the degree of harm remains to be determined. Therein lies one of the dangers. As to traffic in marijuana supporting criminal elements in society, the average young man says, "Come, get with it. Organized crime handles hard drugs; there's no profit in pot. It's available everywhere." While my experience is limited, people of more experience — particularly ex-addicts and the police — seem to disagree with the student.

What are parents and schoolmasters to do about these attitudes? Are drugs just one of those aberrations that suddenly appear among young people and just as suddenly disappear? Or is the problem here to stay? It is difficult to know. Whether or not drugs are a passing aberration, their use is troubling because it is a symptom of a malaise among young persons. If the problems of marijuana are to be met, they must be met in the total context of living, not in isolation.

At St. Albans we shall soon have a visit from a team that is studying the problems of drugs at a local university. A doctor and one or more ex-addicts will speak at Upper and Lower School assemblies sharing a theoretical medical experience and an intensely personal one. Subsequently, the team will make itself available to individuals and small groups of students. In January, the Fathers' Club will present a similar program at a parents' meeting. Furthermore, in the spring we will have a young alumnus, either a lawyer or a law enforcement officer, speak to the boys. None of these programs will be an oratorical fire-and-damnation sermon; rather, each will be a clear, objective statement about drugs and their dangers.

While such programs may be useful, more important are our attitudes and values at home. We cannot offhandedly condemn practices about which we know little and which have never tempted us. Nor can we, aware of the dangers of alcohol and tobacco, pursue practices injurious to our health and well-being. I am all for a home and a school in which there are firm standards, and I believe parents and masters must set them. But I also believe they must be set with understanding and with a sense of responsibility.

Nearly two years ago, following a parent-student meeting

on drugs, I wrote the following words concerning family relationships; they still express my convictions:

> In a session with faculty members, a dean from Yale spoke at length about student-family relationships. He found that the most frequent users of marijuana come either from disturbed homes or from families "without gut involvement." That phrase, although it is not elegant, is expressive. To me, it means without deep and meaningful relationships, without relationships that cost greatly, without emotional involvement, without deep caring.
>
> I think of a family with gut involvement as one in which the father (a fine man) is busy with many responsibilities, unable to spend much time at home — who faces up to family responsibilities (when he must) with a keen mind, meeting problems objectively, making decisions, settling things. The difficulty is that in so doing he seeks to deal with human relationships and nurture a boy in much the same way as he meets business problems. He doesn't realize that one does not settle human problems; one lives through them. A father cannot direct a boy how to grow: he can grow with his son in all his pain and joy, being useful when he is allowed, standing by when he isn't.
>
> Or I think of a family "without gut involvement" as one in which the mother has only a peripheral interest in her children, however much she may protest to the contrary; or as one in which all interests and personalities are such that warm relationships and free communication are difficult. In simplest terms, such a family might be called impersonal.
>
> The basic needs of boys today remain the same as they were yesterday. Boys need acceptance and respect for what they are; boys need to be loved in pain and joy, in failure and success, whether they are lovable or unlovable. Boys need discipline that initially comes from without but that eventually must come from within — self-discipline. These basic requirements are surely more likely to be found in a home in which there is intensity of feeling and depth of relationship than in a home that lacks these characteristics.
>
> I am troubled about what I have just written, for I think at once of the many fine parents whose problems with their children have been severe and painful. Such problems may arise for reasons that are completely beyond our understanding. Regardless of what may be the cause of these problems, I frequently remind parents

that often the boy who has the most difficulty growing up learns the most and develops into the adult who contributes to life far beyond the boy who goes from strength to strength and seems to have no troubles. Still, when these facts are fully recognized, the home that is loving, firm, and strong is the one most likely to nurture the kind of boy who faces alcohol, drugs, and all the other problems of life wisely.

Of this we can be sure — young people of today are no less fine than those of any other generation. Whenever I really meet the mind and spirit of one of our boys — the inner boy — I find honesty, sensitivity, and goodness.

We shall meet the problems of our own young people only as we give ourselves to meeting the problems of all young people — not with a hard, "let's crack down on them," or with an easy permissiveness that fails to recognize evil or personal responsibility, but with an intelligent, compassionate understanding of life and a set of values wrought out of life not only as it was but as it is today. And that is what we are called on to do if we are to be responsible parents to our boys.

Faithfully yours,

Charles Martin

To every thing there is a season, and a time to every purpose under the heaven.

A time to be born, and a time to die: a time to plant, and a time to pluck up that which is planted:

A time to kill, and a time to heal: a time to break down, and time to build up:

A time to weep, and a time to laugh: a time to mourn and a time to dance:

A time to cast away stones, and a time to gather stones together: a time to embrace, and a time to refrain from embracing:

A time to get, and a time to lose: a time to keep, and a time to cast away:

A time to rend, and a time to sew: a time to keep silence, and a time to speak:

A time to love, and a time to hate: a time of war, and a time of peace.

Ecclesiastes 3:1-8

XXXV

There Is a Season

November 6, 1970

Dear Friends,

More than two thousand years ago, a Hebrew preacher wrote these verses. A disillusioned old gentleman, the writer of the book of *Ecclesiastes* was saved from bitterness only through his ultimate trust in God. "Vanity is vanity; all is vanity" is his familiar lament. He speaks at length of the vanity of a man's labor and of how little it profits him, concluding only reluctantly that in labor may be found satisfaction. When such is the case, riches are a gift from God. Furthermore, the writer voices his doubts about the worth of wisdom and study, to which he has given himself assiduously, making an observation with which many a schoolboy would concur: " . . . of making many books there is no end; and much study is a weariness of the flesh." Yet he does acknowledge that wisdom is better than folly. The writer concludes his book with the statement, "Fear God, and keep His commandments: for this is the whole duty of man."

Though weary and disillusioned, this writer finds solace in such poetic insights into the nature of life as the lovely passage that begins, "To every thing there is a season . . . " In these verses, he reveals his ultimate conviction that behind all life is the mystery that gives order and meaning — God.

Recently, when I heard these words from *Ecclesiastes* 3:1-8 set to a hymn and sung by Joan Baez, I was struck by the hauntingly sweet, pure voice of the singer. Although I have always been familiar with the words, I had never given them much thought until I conversed with a group of young people about their meaning. From our discussion I gained new insights that I would like to share with you.

"Why are the recordings of this song so popular?" I asked the group of young persons. "Don't you see?" they answered. "The words mean welcome life, embrace it, plunge in. We want to live fully and not to be mere spectators." I could understand. Interpreted by youth, this passage represents a call to face life with eagerness, to welcome change and a variety of new experiences. Such an interpretation is valid and one to which all of us would do well to give attention, whatever our age.

Those of us who are lonely or timid by nature or who have been hurt by experience are unable to enter into life's fullness. Further, events seem to move at such breakneck speed these days that it is difficult for even the strongest among us to move confidently toward the new. However, to remain flexible and open to life is a condition for meaningful living; if one succumbs to the natural tendency to hold onto what he knows, to retreat into the past, to face the future reluctantly, he dies. All of us — young and old — need to sing hymns that affirm life, allowing us to enter into it with joyousness and courage.

In addition to appreciating the poetry of the song, these young persons felt the verses expressed their feelings about security. They said that however much one welcomes life, it is still natural to be anxious about the future and that it is reassuring as one moves into the uncertainties of life to feel there is rhythm, order, and purpose to living. They observed that it would be equally appropriate to read the passage at a wedding as at a funeral service because the words provide security as one faces the unknown.

Though we did not use the traditional terms God or Providence, the group was expressing intuitively — in its own terms

— the realization that life is not in our hands alone but in God's hands. Such a recognition is essential if we are not to be lost or destroyed by the confusion of the times. In international relations, problems seem to multiply without ever being solved. At home are the problems we ourselves breed — racial bigotry, drugs, poverty, crime, and the revolt of the young. When we listen to the news media, these concerns seem to grow in complexity and intensity.

Deeper still, sometimes unrealized, more often very much recognized, is the possibility that all life may be ended in a nuclear holocaust or that man, in his quest for technological improvement, may destroy his total environment. It is small wonder that our leaders attempt to emphasize the traditional and the good, that the news media are attacked for reporting the troubling rather than the comforting. Yet if we look honestly at our world today, we see self-deception, escape, and ignorance. We need affirmation, rhythm, order, and purpose to counterbalance the negatives.

Implicit in this affirmation is the understanding that we are not masters of our fate, that the seasons and movements of life are often beyond our ken. Those close to nature, like that fast disappearing breed — the farmer — have always known that winds and storms, droughts and plagues, visit us but also depart. It is for the farmer to cope with nature by understanding it as best he can, by cooperating with its seasons and forces. He does not make his crops grow; he understands and cooperates with the natural life that enables them to grow.

Problems with ourselves and with our children that appear unsolvable will not be solved by us alone — if, indeed, they are solved. Rather they must be seen as being a part of the rhythm, movement, and inscrutable order of life. Some problems we can help to solve, but only if we have the love, wisdom, and humility to cooperate with nature and its seasons, if we do not try to play God. Let us lay aside our frenetic worries and anxieties; let us relax and seek to cooperate with forces beyond our understanding.

To lay aside the familiar and face the new with confidence, to take time out to enjoy our family and friends, to appreciate nature around us, to shed the fears with which we face the future, to recognize that we ourselves cannot solve all problems, to believe the words of Ecclesiastes — why, this is the good news. This is the Gospel!

Faithfully yours,

Charles Martin

Strolling with Cleopatra IV, 1970's.

Human life is reduced to real suffering, to hell, only when two ages, two cultures and religions overlap . . . . There are times when a whole generation is caught in this way between two ages, two modes of life, with the consequences that it loses all power to understand itself and has no standard, no security, no simple acquiescence.

Herman Hesse, Steppenwolf

XXXVI

Three Boys—Growing to Manhood

February 19, 1971

Dear Friends,

This letter concerns three boys. Each is a composite rather than a real boy, but — in a sense — all are real. They could be your boy, my boy, our boys.

David has been causing us much concern. He is no longer the happy boy we once knew; he now has few friends at School and is doing poorly in his studies. Although School presents problems, matters at home are far worse. There is constant friction about hair, dress, manners, and friends. The once pleasant household is continually upset. Dinner is a time of battle or of sullen quiet; evenings are a time of argument over studies, the telephone, or TV. Old friends no longer drop in at the house; new friends are spoken to on the telephone or met oustide the house. David's parents think his new friends are "hippies" with undesirable manners. As far as they know, drugs are not in the picture, but his parents certainly fear them.

David, his parents, and I have held lengthy consultations about boarding schools, public school, and new regimens here. No course has yet been settled upon. Seemingly more mature than his contemporaries, David has sought older friends. He has turned to boys in his neighborhood for companionship because, like him, they are uneasy and troubled; they find comfort in their common uneasiness. Yet the interests they are pursuing are not approved of by his parents. David's world and that of his parents differ widely. His family lives formally with a clear set of values. On the contrary, David's life is informal; he has few definite values. His lifestyle is derived from books, films, and music as well as from conversations with friends with whom he spends much time.

David has long since ceased trying to communicate with his parents. They do not — perhaps cannot — listen or understand. "Rock music is dreadful noise," they say. "You call that dancing?" "How can you enjoy movies like that?" David openly flouts the values his family holds high. His parents' love is expressed through worried efforts to change things. Yet the situation is in a stalemate.

What of the future? Who can say? Most problems are outlived. There may come a hurt severe enough that the eyes of David's parents will be opened or David will be so "shook up" that he will understand. Someone, perhaps a girl, may touch David and he may begin to see his parents in a new light. What is important at the moment is that relations be maintained, that his parents somehow learn to overlook the unimportant and be open to and tolerant of the new and the strange. From experience, I know that out of rough times like these often come understandings among family members that are richer than when life goes along more quietly and smoothly.

Now let us look at Bill. Out of school for two days, ostensibly ill, Bill stayed home because of an argument with his parents. He refused to go to school, and he was too big to be forced. This was not the first row but one in a long series. At issue was Bill's general appearance — long hair, beads, and the like. The preceding summer had been one of family explosions and reconciliations, with two short periods when Bill had run away. Listening to his parents, I began to understand. Bill was his father's son.

Bill's father had left high school before graduation to make his own way in life. Up and down the country, in and out of jobs, in the Army, he had lived and learned. Formal education had come at the end of this hard but valuable basic education. Business and financial success followed, but the values of Bill's father hardened and became more conservative; they varied markedly from those of his son. Bill's father is determined that his son be spared his own painful experiences, know all the advantages he lacked, and have the best possible education.

Like his father thirty years before, Bill wants to make his own way at his own speed without anyone telling him how to do it. Two such strong wills bring frequent explosions, followed by short periods of peace but longer periods of separation. Bill's mother is understanding; she has a sense of humor. In her is a hope from her healthy perspective on life. Ultimately Bill will grow in his own way.

Jim, our third boy, did well at St. Albans, holding several responsible positions. He enjoyed much success in art and music, and we all were proud of him when he graduated. In the middle of his first year in college, however, he disappeared; weeks later he turned up living in a commune. Today he is drifting. We hear of him occasionally from his classmates. Jim's dropping out amazed us, but with hindsight we began to understand. An able, sensitive boy, he had gone along doing things expected of him. He had worked hard, often under great tension. Freed from the pressures of conforming to what was expected of him by parents and school, of drivenness in his studies, of standards he rejected, he rebelled against what to him seemed like more of the same.

Perhaps we should have seen the pressures and the need to relieve them. Perhaps we should have recommended that Jim take a year off between school and college. He needed time — as do so many boys — to let his emotions and experiences catch up with his intellect. He needed time to test his values against those of the real world. And we at St. Albans needed the wisdom and sensitivity to help him grow, to prepare him for life — not merely outwardly but inwardly. I believe that Jim will come through, but at the cost of great pain. I also believe that because of his painful experiences, he will have greater sensitivity and understanding toward others. I do not know if we could have spared him this experience.

Am I saying that all boys have troubles? Yes. And no. Some resemble David, Bill, and Jim. Other boys seem to go along successfully, happily, with only the most sensitive among us being aware of their inner tumults. Occasionally their long-concealed problems burst out. More often, however, things are worked out, adjustments are made, and few others are aware of their difficulty. Then there are those boys who go along uneventfully, do their jobs, and are quite happy — or so it seems.

Growing into manhood has never been easy; pain and hurt are essential to growth. Those who are the most sensitive know the greatest pain — even hell. Yet out of the hell of pain and difficulty often emerges the greatest good. The finest of man's creation rarely emerges during times of stability or in lives of contentment and ease; it emerges in times of crisis and pain, in lives that are restless and hurt. In hell even as in heaven there is God. Indeed, most often through suffering do we know Him. In our irritations and frustrations with our Davids, Bills, or Jims, it may not be easy for us to see that they may ultimately come to know the good of God himself — yet they often do.

In the words of the Teacher, "Blessed are the meek: for they shall inherit the earth." In the language of today, happy are those who are humble, open, able to learn the new. They shall know a life that is rich, full, and good. "Blessed are the merciful: for they shall obtain mercy." Or happy and rich in life are those who are sympathetic, compassionate, and understanding; those qualities shall be returned to them. "Blessed are they which do hunger and thirst after righteousness: for they shall be filled." Or, happy are they who unceasingly search for the right, lay aside the form, and hold to the substance. They shall be fulfilled and even know God.

As we live with humility and compassion, always searching for the right with our Davids, Bills, and Jims, we can — even in the midst of great confusion (even because of it) grow into finer, better human beings ourselves and so help our children to become better, finer human beings.

Faithfully yours,

Charles Martin

We thank Thee, O God,

For the ability to do more, the more we do,

For the courage that can come out of failure,

For the knowledge that all things work together for good to them that love the Lord.

Grant that we may show forth our thanks not only with our lips but also in our lives;

Through Jesus Christ our Lord. Amen.

Adapted by Charles Martin

XXXVII

Thank God for Our Problems

January 19, 1972

Dear Friends,

Although this letter was composed on New Year's Day, it is not a resolution. It is both a greeting and an attempt to put into writing certain understandings about life that I believe can be useful to us in our relations with boys — indeed, in all human relationships.

Let me begin with a quotation from a sermon, the best sermon I have heard in years. It is one sentence long: "Thank God for our problems." Perhaps because at the time I heard the quotation I was endeavoring to understand a problem, but more likely because of its fundamental truth, the sermon caused me to think with unusual clarity. I left the service a better human being.

The truth of the sermon lies largely in the fact that the problems of life put demands on us that develop within us strengths previously unknown, leading to new understandings and appreciations of life that not only make the problems more bearable but also make life richer.

A parent whose husband had recently died told me when I visited her, "I had no idea I had so many friends. People have been so kind. The house has been crowded with neighbors offering help, the kitchen is full of food; messages have come from people I hardly know." Through the experience, she has found strength within herself as well as a new understanding of and appreciation for people and for life itself.

At the beginning of winter athletics, a member of a varsity squad was injured. The goal toward which he had worked all fall, toward which he had hoped and dreamed all year seemed to have vanished. The depth of his disappointment is difficult to appreciate unless you have suffered such a blow yourself. The hurt, frustration, and disappointment were clearly visible in the boy, even though he tried to gloss over these painful emotions with a "that's the breaks" attitude. Now one sees signs that the boy is changing. Through the thoughtfulness of some friends, he is finding satisfaction in art and — now that time is abundant — learning that even math can be fun. My guess is that he will sort out his values, develop strengths he did not know he had, and come to athletics next year better equipped to cope with games and with life.

I remember a mother who suffered fears and anxieties about her boy who was involved in all forms of athletics. At the end of a football game, more exhausted than her son, she would say, "Thank God, one more game is over!" Off the athletic field, this mother spent much time with masters worrying about why her son — a boy of solid academic ability — was doing only mediocre work. I imagine that at home there were the usual problems of social life and of growing up that were even more worrisome to her. Then, at one of the holiday parties a few days ago, I saw our mother (her son is now in Vietnam), and we reminisced. As I left her she said, "Those were the richest days of my life — and did I learn!" She did, and so did we all. We learned patience and understanding and found richer meanings in life.

I do not mean to suggest that death and accidents, disappointments and frustrations, fears and anxieties represent the whole of life. Happily they do not. But they *are* a normal part of day-to-day living. And fortunately they often teach us qualities that make living most worthwhile: sympathy and wisdom, patience and love.

However, our lives become richer and we gain strength only as we realize that the problems of human relationships are not solved in the manner we so often assume — in a logical fashion, by turning to experts, or even through the good old American virtue of hard work. Even though we may be determined to make things come out the way we want or expect them to, human beings are too complex, to unpredictable, and too full of mystery for problems to be solved neatly and efficiently. To some of our problems there are only limited answers; to other, there appear to be no answers at all. This does not mean that we should not work to find solutions, taking advantage of all the expert help available. Indeed, we must always be seeking answers with all our skill and patience. However, when all is said and done, some problems must be endured. Neat solutions and tidy outcomes are rarely, if ever, attainable. And often the answers that do come are quite different from those we had anticipated, the result not only of our efforts but also of Providence, of life in all its mystery.

I like the point of view of a friend who says, "We were fortunate with our children. We had no problems." This statement represents both nonsense and absolute truth. Nonsense: My friend's children had all the problems of any other children. I remember how he and his wife sensitively, wisely, and lovingly opened up a shy child to the world, helping her to go to school, meet people, accept life. I also remember how the father sweated out an athletic ceremony, knowing full well that, although his son had worked hard to receive a letter, he would not receive one. He helped the boy accept that disappointment. Absolute truth: My friend and his wife never regarded their daughter's or son's limitations as problems. Rather, they regarded them as part of living. A parent helped when he could, suffered when he could not help, and occasionally just lived through the difficulties that seemed to have no solutions.

Yet I am troubled by the fact that what I have said sounds somewhat simplistic, much too neat and pat. While it is always easy to say what should be done, it is ever so difficult to do it. Still, I have seen hundreds of parents and boys who verify my words and my experiences.

Baskets of Christmas cards on my desk are alive with vivid

memories. One comes from a tense, anxious, driven boy — one of that sizable troubled group called perfectionists. I remember taking him out of a course to relieve pressures, suggesting he go to bed early, forbidding him to study over weekends, getting a friend to take him to baseball games on Saturdays. A note on his card suggests that he is still a perfectionist and always will be, but he is learning to live with himself. Another boy who failed in his studies and was remote from his parents responded to none of the tricks of the trade. Parents and masters alike were worried; so was the boy. But time and a patient, loving girl helped the boy's problems; fortitude and wisdom enabled his parents to live through the experience. I could go on with examples, but enough.

May your New Year be rich and joyous, made so by the wonderful experience of facing with your boy his problems and experiences, not by expecting easy answers but by living through them with patience, courage, wisdom, humility, and love.

Faithfully yours,

Charles Martin

From the excessive demands of business and social life that limit family relationships,

From the insensitivity and harshness of judgment that prevent understanding,

From domineering ways and selfish imposition of our will,

From softness and indulgence mistaken for love,

Good Lord, deliver us.

Charles Martin

XXXVIII

Are We Too Busy?

April 12, 1973

Dear Friends,

This morning in chapel we dedicated a plaque to the memory of Sam Hoffman, an extraordinary man who served St. Albans for many years both as a teacher and as a coach. Only a few boys were seated, so I waited for more to arrive. After a few moments, however, I realized that all who were coming were present. There was a long and heavy silence as I waited for a colleague to come up to the lectern to deliver a tribute to Sam. I found my colleague still in his chair, overcome by emotion. Recognizing that he would be unable to deliver the tribute, I completed the service. Later, several faculty members expressed to me their disappointment over so few boys having attended the memorial service. To each of them — only partially believing what I said — I replied that few students had really known Sam well.

Yet I have been pondering the experience all day. So few boys in chapel . . . so soon forgotten . . . I am not overly critical of the boys, realizing that they had been busy with their early morning concerns. However, I am critical of society in general. We do so little to help young people to be sensitive to others and to appreciate what others have done for them.

All of us keep so busy that there is little time for us to develop relationships and enjoy people, let alone to recognize and appreciate all the "givens" in life. And we are barely aware of that dimension in life that enables us to live with the memory and in the spirit of those who have gone before us. When death comes, we are often at a loss to know how to meet it. As a people, we seem to discourage remembering the dead — even saints and heroes. Anniversaries of George Washington's or Abraham Lincoln's birth or a memorial day to those who have died for their country are occasions for long weekends of relaxation, with no time set aside to remember or to give thanks. Why should I or the faculty have been surprised that so few boys were in chapel? Indeed, we should have expected it.

The great historic forces of our time of rapid change, complexity, and impersonality make it difficult for us to develop relationships with the living, much less with the dead. As our population explodes, human relationships decrease; as our life becomes more urban, we lose our association with all of nature. We cover the earth with buildings and with highways of cement and asphalt; we race along them too fast to enjoy the countryside; thus, we grow ever more remote from the earth and all its life and beauty. We need association with people — intense, intimate. We need the care and love of animals; we need the earth, sky, and sea; we need the past as well as the present. If we do not know The Life that is in and through all life, then our lives become dull, fragmented, limited, and hopelessly incomplete.

Happily, there are signs that we are realizing our impoverishment of spirit. Among our young people we see a searching for new values, new modes of living. Our boys at school are interested in and concerned about the outdoors — from backpacking and camping to concern about the environment. A new devotion to and participation in all the arts make the traditional schoolmaster draw back in surprise. Boys want to cultivate the beautiful and to express themselves in painting, music, drama, and creative writing. The rigidly followed pattern of the past — school, college, graduate school, then business or profession — is being questioned and occasionally abandoned as young people search for more rewarding relationships and a more satisfying life than they witness in the world around them. Some seek unconventional religious disciplines in their effort to know and experience greater awareness of life, an inner quiet, or a new order and meaning in life. Such searching is not, however, confined to the young. Though this quest is more obvious among them, it is common to our times and true of our generation as well.

Yet while we seek the new, we still need to embrace customs and practices from the past. One of these is the observation of the season through which we are now passing and that has, throughout the centuries, had much meaning but is now little observed — Lent. For all of us, regardless of our religious backgrounds, the central ideas of Lent — drawing back from busyness, being quiet, being aware of people, of life, and of God — are still valid. Indeed, the extraordinary changes of our times make Lent and its practices more, not less, contemporary. We all need a season in which we can listen to the quiet of the earth and hear the stirrings of life in all its diversity and abundance, to look at one blossom or at one bird and feel and know in them the mystery of life . . . to listen to the past and hear it speak . . . to listen to a friend and hear him through his words, action, and silence . . . to listen to all life and see the transcendent.

As my thoughts return to the chapel service this morning, I see more clearly what St. Albans can do. We can help our boys not only to do well in academics, but also — and even more important — to become more aware of, more sensitive to, more grateful for people and for life itself.

To this end, we shall be joining more fully the movement to humanize life, so visible among today's young people. We shall be keeping more fully in mind The Teacher who suggests that it does not matter how many boys win the National Merit Scholarships or what colleges they attend if their lives are not rich and full. "For what is a man profited if he shall gain the whole world, and lose his own soul?"

Faithfully yours,

Charles Martin

Almighty God, who has given us this good land for our heritage, we humbly beseech thee that we may always prove ourselves a people mindful of thy favor and glad to do thy will.

Bless our land with honorable industry, sound learning, and pure manners. Save us from violence, discord, and confusion; from pride and arrogance, and from every evil way.

Defend our liberties, and fashion into one united people the multitudes brought hither out of many kindreds and tongues. Endue with the spirit of wisdom those to whom in thy name we entrust the authority of government that there may be justice and peace at home, and that, through obedience to thy law, we may show forth thy praise among the nations of the earth. In times of prosperity, fill our hearts with thankfulness, and in the day of trouble, suffer not our trust in thee to fail; all which we ask, we ask through Jesus Christ our Lord.

*Charles Martin**

---

*This prayer was originally published in the St. Albans Alumni *Bulletin*, Spring 1961.

XXXIX

The Why of Watergate

September 5, 1973

Dear Friends,

Though much of importance has happened at St. Albans over the summer, the most significant event occurred not at St. Albans but at Watergate. We are understandably tired of the very sound of the word and would wish the whole business away, but we know we cannot. We have to live with the events and draw lessons from them. To that end, I would like to make some observations about what Watergate means to our School.

Just before the end of last term, three boys engaged in a heated argument about Watergate came to see me for my opinion on the matter. Though we talked for over an hour, we resolved nothing. At the lunch table, Watergate has come up for discussion almost daily. Always there have been such comments as "incredible," "they ought to be sent to jail," "the Committee is making a mountain out of a molehill," "there has been nothing like it in our history," or "such practices have always gone on." Yet there has been no consensus among students as there was a few years ago on the many subjects that had separated generations.

Faculty reactions—though expressed more fully and thoughtfully—have been of much the same tenor, although they were expressed as a restless desire to take action. For those who have felt dissatisfied with our society's moral attitudes or who have felt a vague discontent within themselves about their lives, Watergate has acted as a catalyst. Sometimes the action it has precipitated has been wise, sometimes unwise.

Only recently, a very respected teacher submitted his resignation to me. With obvious pain, he explained that he was at St. Albans not just to teach a subject but to help boys who would be tomorrow's leaders be more sensitive, more aware of the right than his own generation had been. When this master saw young men from the same social and economic background as our boys appear before the Senate Committee, he decided St. Albans was not for him. He felt that he had to get away from Washington and find some other useful vocation. I tried to dissuade him, citing comments from boys and parents about what he has meant to them, but the trauma surrounding Watergate was too great; he would not listen.

Other masters, troubled in varying degrees, have come into my study just to talk. A few have questioned their effectiveness with young people. However, their general reaction has been that of most other troubled citizens, but with a strong conviction that we must look at ourselves and at what we are doing here at School. Are we holding high the values we know are right in our own lives? In the lives of our boys? Some faculty members have expressed the concern that in spite of our desire to understand and meet the individual needs of each boy, we have failed to hold him firmly to values we know to be good; thus, we have done him not a kindness but an injustice.

In the light of Watergate, other learning institutions across the nation have been examining themselves. The dean of a school of education, writing in *The New York Times*, stated that Watergate clearly shows that we have failed in education: We are not raising up informed, intellectually able students; hence, we must revise our curricula if we are not to continue to fail. I agree with the dean that we must give our students the opportunity both in and out of school to develop their abilities to the fullest, for only by doing so will they have a sense of well-being. Young people caught up in interests that extend their abilities will be those who are fulfilled and who are likely to move purposefully into further education and into later life. But I profoundly disagree that education must look only to turning out brighter, better informed, more intellectual students. Watergate must not move us in education to another spurt of disciplined effort akin to that caused by Sputnik. Nor must we believe that the answers to Watergate lie in schools alone. Too often we look to education as a solution for all of society's ills; of course, it never is. The answers that lie in education are much more complex than offering more and better courses with ever higher standards to more and better young people for ever-longer periods of time. Although there was no paucity of well-informed, able young men involved in Watergate, there *was* a paucity of honesty, truth, and integrity.

St. Albans School and education in general must do something about that paucity. We cannot do it through courses in ethics. We can teach honesty, truth, and integrity in our common life—through values that individual masters hold high and values the School holds high. Bringing this about is not nearly as simple as teaching a subject. In today's world, truth, honesty, and integrity are difficult to determine in any given situation. I think of the comparatively simple judgments I must make when a boy comes to me with a problem. At such times I am painfully aware that what is wholly honest, wholly true, and wholly right is rarely clear; but so far as it is given to us to understand these values, we must be wholly and unflinchingly committed to them. Obviously, such virtues cannot be nurtured by the School alone but must grow out of the life of the home, the community, and society at large.

Without trying to make one more analysis of the "why" of Watergate, it is clear that part of the problem is that we as a people have been confusing means and ends, often justifying any means to accomplish an end that seemed right. Such a way of thinking has grown out of long and common practices that most clearly began during World War II. We fought fire with fire, bombing with bombing, spying with spying, dirty tricks with dirty tricks. At the end of the war, peace simply moved us from hot to cold war.

The thirty years of cold war were interrupted not by periods of peace but by the hot wars of Korea and Vietnam. Truth—a casualty of any war—was lost for so long that none of us, not merely the principals in Watergate, has found it easy to recognize or abide by. That goodness begets goodness; honesty begets honesty; understanding begets understanding; and love, the most powerful force in the world, begets love—these truths have either been forgotten or judged to be naive and weak. Values unclear or ignored, means and ends confused—these have been the norms operating among us for a generation. "Among us" I write deliberately. We must not forget that it was not the Nazi party or a small group of vicious people who were guilty of the Dachaus of Germany. The collective responsibility for Nazism rested with the whole German people, for they allowed the evil to come into being and thus shared in the guilt. Watergate is therefore a judgment not alone on those who appear on TV but on all Americans, including you and me.

A sermon delivered by Rev. John Coburn at St. James' Church in New York City early this summer spoke to me about Watergate with discernment and force. In this sermon, Rev. Coburn told of the ancient walled city of Jerusalem that had several gates, one of which, by the Spring of Gihon, was the Water Gate. In about 445 B.C., the people gathered by this gate for a ceremony that was to remind them of their responsibilities before God. Before those assembled (including Nehemiah, the Governor) Ezra, the Priest, read from the Scriptures. He reminded all those assembled that their loyalty to their country could be expressed only as loyalty to God—that meant obedience to God's law of righteousness and justice. The day of the assembly was a holy day, and the ceremonies developed into the Feast of Tabernacles, still observed as a holy day by the Jewish people. This festival is made holy not by God but by the people through their loyalty to God's laws of justice, truth, and righteousness.

As a nation, we stand before our Watergate, judged by God Himself. America's Watergate can be holy only if we make it so. God does not bless America; we bless God by obedience to his laws of justice and truth. Then, and only then, does God bless America. Our responsibility at St. Albans is to help bless America by recognizing with greater clarity that we must hold firmly to truth, honesty, and justice. I believe this process has begun at St. Albans. I pray that we may have the wisdom and strength to carry it forward.

Faithfully yours,

Charles Martin

We have associated simplicity with poverty, but we have discovered that affluence without simplicity is a giant trap. Every saint who ever lived, lived simply, not because he was holier but because he was smarter.

Eric Sevareid, Commentary

XL

Crisis—Energy

November 26, 1973

Dear Friends,

A recent issue of *The Washington Post* pictured an Amish farmer traveling placidly along the road in a horse-drawn cart followed by a fuel truck forced to the pace of the horses. The caption read, "Amish Farmer Asks, 'What Energy Crisis?' " That photograph suggests we have much to learn from the current crisis: humility, simplicity, and a love and respect for the earth.

In an effort to conserve fuel at School, we are seeking to keep temperatures between 65 and 68 degrees. To do so is difficult because our several different heating systems range from those with sophisticated thermostatic control to those with antiquated no-control; more important, because we humans and our habits are difficult to change and control. It is evident that we will be able to conserve fuel at St. Albans not merely by decree but by education born of necessity.

Important as it is for us to conserve fuel—and we will—it is much more important for us to realize that the energy crisis means we are moving into a way of life markedly different from that we have known. We must educate ourselves to prepare for the changes that shortages of our natural resources will engender. The news media are full of dark forebodings about what directions lie ahead. These predictions are natural, for fear of the unknown causes anxiety, and there is no doubt that difficulties do lie ahead. Still I believe that our problems lie in our having had too much affluence rather than too much austerity. It would be helpful if we could predict the future and see clearly the nature of the forthcoming changes, but none of us is gifted with that kind of prescience. Of this I feel certain: the new way of life will surely bear some of the elements implicit in the picture of the Amish farmer and his cart—simplicity, love of nature, and firm religious values.

It is good for us to learn to cope with some adversity. Even as you and I adopt ways to conserve and simplify, so will our boys embrace new values—simple but important ones. They will understand, for example, that books are valuable and cannot be idly marked up or casually left about but are to be cared for and, after careful use, sold second-hand. All kinds of personal belongings—one's own and others'—will be valued and cared for properly. Perhaps walking and biking will replace the taken-for-granted automobile ride. We may rediscover some of the simpler, less expensive satisfactions of life.

Our Valedictorian, Henry Shattuck Richardson, was not thinking about the Amish when he delivered the Valedictory Address at Prize Day last June, but in his speech he stressed the need for limits to growth. The address was most impressive when delivered; in the light of what has happened recently, it is even more impressive now. I believe you will find the following excerpts from his address helpful and interesting as they apply to our energy crisis:

> Look within yourselves and ask yourselves whether your happiness must be tied to material abundance .... I would exhort you to formulate a contingency plan to cover yourself in the event that our posh existence is wrested from us. I am almost moved to urge you to look to the wilderness .... There you can be alone, yet not lonely, for everywhere around you the miracle of life is going on in its fullest, and you will feel humble in the face of God's creation. But I know that you will all have to find your own sources of happiness, whether they be in the love of your companions or in serving goals greater than yourselves ....

> I am not telling you to eat, drink, and be merry for tomorrow you may die. Eat, drink, and be merry by all means; but also use well the skills you have learned here in school so that if crisis is avoidable it may be avoided.
>
> I wish for you: grace, to meet the crisis with honor and without bitterness if it comes, and inner peace, so that even if the GNP cannot grow, your happiness can.

In the meantime, we at St. Albans will do our best to conserve fuel. More important, however, we will seek to prepare for a future in which simplicity in lifestyles, a love of nature, and a love for the Lord in all life may become more significant than it is today.

Faithfully yours,

Charles Martin

O God, who in the mystery of Thy providence has brought us together in a common responsibility for St. Albans School, keep us from a false sense of values and from confusing means and ends.

Help us to give of ourselves, of our time, and of our substance, without counting the cost, seeking only to be open and receptive to Thy Spirit that we may give and labor not in vain, but to Thy glory. All of which we ask through Jesus Christ, our Lord. Amen.

Charles Martin

XLI

Resignation of a President

August 9, 1974

Dear Friends,

Last evening as I watched TV, waiting for the speech in which the President would announce his resignation, a sense of uneasiness and loneliness caused me to telephone all my children. I suppose in solemn moments such as these we all need to share our feelings with those close to us. As I continued to watch the proceedings, I often wondered what our students were doing, always hoping that they were sharing in this—one of the most poignant moments of American history. Had I been able to, I would have telephoned each one of you. Instead, I planned to write to you after the President's address to say what I would have said in chapel had school been in session.

The momentous evening is over. As I write, it is chapel time. Vice President Ford is just leaving his home for the White House. Last evening was for me profoundly sad and yet profoundly satisfying. I saw the pain and hurt of the President and his family and the terrible anguish through which our country has passed. At the same time, I saw the great pride and satisfaction in the strength of our institutions and our people. Just a few years ago there was widespread restlessness, particularly among young people, over the inability of our governmental processes to function. Now, in a great crisis, those processes have vindicated themselves. And our people have proved themselves. Throughout the long, painful workings of justice, our institutions have remained strong and our people steadfast, uncovering truth through their representatives while at the same time carrying on with their private responsibilities. We can be very proud. Learning from what has happened, confident in our newfound strength, we can support our new President and move toward our best vision of America.

Constantly in my thoughts last evening was a visit I had had just before School closed with a family who had been deeply involved in Watergate. Much self-conscious small talk covered the uneasiness each of us felt with our shared knowledge that the father of the family would be sentenced the next day. As we parted, the mother touched my arm and said, "Pray for us." I could have wept.

The next morning I went to chapel and tried to order my thoughts so that I could pray. Slowly it became clear to me that whatever pain the man and his family would suffer, justice had to be done. It was also clear that it was not for me to condemn. The crimes of Watergate were not the crimes of one individual; rather they were the crimes of us all. While there was individual guilt, there was also collective guilt. Winning at any cost, using the end to justify the means, accepting easily what we knew was not right—these are common failings among us. I could not condemn, for I was among the guilty. My heart could go out to the family, and I could pray that they and I might see the right and hold to it today, tomorrow, and forevermore.

As I prayed, verses from Psalm 139 came to mind:

> O Lord, Thou hast searched me, and known me.
>
> Thou knowest my downsitting and mine uprising; Thou understandeth my thoughts afar off . . . .
>
> If I ascend up into heaven, Thou art there:
> if I make my bed in hell, behold, Thou art there . . . .
>
> If I say, Surely the darkness shall cover me; even the night shall be light about me.

> Yea, the darkness hideth not from Thee: but the night shineth as the day: the darkness and the light are both alike to Thee.

In the quiet of the chapel I knew that wherever we are, whatever we do, God is present. He is in persons, in events, in nature—in all of life. In Him we can know the right and find the strength to do it. I prayed that the Watergate family might find among their friends and in the Church the Presence that sustains and enables good to come out of even the deepest tragedy. I prayed that they might know that "the darkness hideth not from Thee."

We can be proud of our country and its search for truth and justice; we can also suffer with those who are suffering. In this and in all experience let us seek to be open to Him who can enable us to have the wisdom to know and the strength to do what is right.

Faithfully yours,

Charles Martin

Almighty God, through the mystery of your holy church you have given us a means of understanding the mystery of creation and through that mystery of the Incarnation you have helped us to fathom the mystery of leadership. Help us we pray through the power of the Holy Spirit to guide others into a deeper and more profound sense of purpose and leadership on earth through your son, Jesus Christ Our Lord. Amen.

*Bishop John T. Walker**

*The Right Reverend John T. Walker has served as Bishop of Washington from 1977 to the present and as Dean of the Washington Cathedral from 1978 to the present.

XLII

The Mystery of Leadership

August 30, 1974

Dear Friends,

"In the top third of his class at Yale Law School." This headline in a column about President Ford in a recent newspaper expressed to me the idea that the President is a complex person who cannot be stereotyped by a simplistic image as a Midwesterner or by his past record in Congress. It was a good column, emphasizing a truth easily overlooked. The President—like every human being—is infinitely complex, and any image of him is bound to be imperfect—even false. No man is wholly what he seems, even to those who know him best. In all of us there are unexpected strengths and weaknesses, unrecognized qualities and abilities. Always there is a person beyond full comprehension.

It is good for us to keep this fact well in mind as we begin a new school year. As parents and teachers, we must free ourselves from facile categorizations and images of our boys and, with open minds, seek to discern their individuality and to nurture that individuality with love, understanding, and strength—never forgetting, however, that there is always more to a boy than we can ever know.

Related to the mystery of personality is the mystery of leadership, the unpredictability of responsibilities one may be called upon to assume. Throughout the deliberations of the Judiciary Committee, over which the chairman presided with such dignity and fairness, I kept thinking of the happenstances of life that brought this son of an Italian immigrant, raised in humble circumstances and with a relatively unexceptional career in Congress, to a position of such enormous prominence and historical significance. Similarly, one thinks with wonder of President Ford, who had promised his wife that he would retire and whose greatest ambition had been to become Speaker of the House. He could not have dreamed that the Presidency would be thrust upon him. These men could not have imagined the responsibilities that would come to them, the burden of leadership that would be theirs.

We cannot know what responsibilities, what positions of leadership our boys may have to assume. What we do know is that we have a duty so to nurture our boys that they may bear their responsibilities with grace and dignity. Some speak easily of training potential leaders, of schools for the elite that will accomplish this purpose. There is an element of pretension in these facile assumptions about such schools that makes me uncomfortable. Leaders cannot be trained. A school may help students to develop their gifts or to develop a sense of responsibility in the use of those gifts so that, if occasion demands, they may use them for purposes of leadership. As a school we can do no more than that. We should do no less.

An experience I had this summer illustrates the theme of this letter, and I would like to recount it to you. I have known Michael Collins '48 for a number of years, yet not until I read *Carrying the Fire*, his account of his life from boy to astronaut, did I really meet the man whom I had thought I had known for so long. Over and over again as I read the book I said to myself, "Martin, how stupid can you be! Martin, Martin, what a slow learner you are! Will you never learn to go beneath the surface and meet the real person? Will you never learn that you can't ever really know anyone completely?"

As I read, I came to understand to some degree the height and depth, the richness and uniqueness of the experience that had been Mike's and the difficulties that he must have had as he re-entered what is to us "normal life." Further, I realized—insofar as I could—the awful loneliness he must have felt during his space journey on Apollo 11. I understood Mike as I had not before, and I believe I shall be less likely in the future to take any boy, any person, any leader, at face value.

A challenging year awaits the School. We shall be making plans to join the nation's celebration of its Bicentennial. Because of our long period of national anguish, a new atmosphere of healing, trust, and hope exists. So it is with each new school term. As one of our masters reminds me perennially, "How wonderful it is to be in a profession that affords a new, clean start each year!" I look forward to sharing with you that deeply satisfying, even thrilling, experience of watching and helping the unique personality of your boy to unfold as he prepares to make his own contribution to life.

Blessings on you and on our new School year.

Faithfully yours,

Charles Martin

Almighty God, we give Thee thanks for family life; for its responsibilities and duties that make for strength and courage; for its companionship and shared interests that bring security and fullness to life; for its love that understands and nourishes, brings joy and inner peace.

More especially, O Lord, we praise Thee for mothers; for their patience and constant caring; for their love that unites the family and blesses the home.

May Thy love among us be deepened and made ever more strong so that our families may be useful to Thee and to Thy larger family of which we are all a part. We ask this through Him who came that we might have life and have it more abundantly, Jesus Christ, Our Lord. Amen.

Charles Martin

XLIII

Mothers and Family Life

May 9, 1976

Dear Friends,

This letter, written on Mother's Day, is a series of reflections on motherhood. Several recent events have caused me to focus on mothers and to reflect upon those who know the deepest relationships in life and who are the heart of a group that still is, and I hope will always be, the basis of our society—the family.

This winter our parent suppers honored former chairwomen of our Mothers' Club, from its establishment twenty-two years ago until the present. The mothers present enjoyed reminiscing about the early years of the Club. At the Lower School supper, we even created a mother. After having served the School as secretary for forty-seven years, with hundreds of boys swirling around her and hundreds of mothers consulting her, Miss Virginia Martin was named an honorary member of the Mothers' Club. Quite a distinction for a single lady!

Last week I gave the invocation at the Annual Banquet for American Mothers. I went reluctantly, for it had been a busy week, and my thoughts were elsewhere. As is so often the case, however, what I did reluctantly I enjoyed thoroughly. President Ford was present; I found it refreshing to see him relaxed and untroubled by the heavy demands of his office. The address of the evening, given by the Senior Editor of *Reader's Digest*, was thought provoking and closed with a stirring religious peroration that made me believe that even I could help to forge a better world. Most of all, I enjoyed seeing the mothers, who represented our fifty states.

One of those whom the event honored was a grandmother of two of our boys. This lady had ten children, fifty grandchildren, and eight great-grandchildren. I pondered this astonishing fact, wondering how she could know them all. Was she able to remember each of their names? Then I recalled the members of her family with whom I am acquainted; I thought I could see in them the same sparkle and energy that she possessed. I could then understand how she was able to know each of her family members and know them well.

Before the banquet, I visited with a man from Pennsylvania who was to escort his mother to her place of honor at the head table. He happened to be a member of a parish outside Philadelphia with which I was familiar. We shared pleasant memories about a number of mutual friends. What I really enjoyed was seeing his love for and pride in his mother. During dinner as I watched her at the table, I saw in her dignity, graciousness, and character.

The next morning, our chapel speaker presented the third in a series of homilies on family life. His long preamble was filled with a natural, easy wit that the boys loved. Interspersed were a number of cleverly phrased remarks about the breakdown of the family and the harm that mothers sometimes do their children. He spoke further about the rebellion children often naturally feel toward their parents and toward other family members. The talk was so long, so sophisticated, and so negative that I became irritated. At that point, the speaker closed his talk with a bang in two minutes using these words, "You have to forgive; you have to realize that your parents are human and that they make mistakes just as you do. When you learn to forgive, you begin to understand your parents, and you begin to love and to know that you are loved beyond your deserving, even as God loves you." The clergyman's talk was very humbling and effective. It touched the boys.

After the chapel service, I could not help but reflect upon the difference between the ideas about motherhood presented at the previous night's dinner and in chapel. Although the presentations seemed to be worlds apart, each gave a picture of motherhood that was essentially true. The mothers who had been honored at the dinner had grown up at another time, raised their families in another world, lived by a different set of values than those of today—values rich in religious convictions. Our boys are growing up in an age of great cultural change and uncertain standards; religion often seems to lack meaning in their lives. Our chapel speaker knew this. He reached the boys through his wit and his awareness of their ambivalent feelings toward family life. Thus, he succeeded in opening their minds to an abiding truth—that love is the essence of life. Nowhere is that love more fully expressed than in mothers and in the family. His message was that love is undeserved and comes freely from the Lord. Only as we are able to forgive and are able to express love openly can we come to know God's love.

During the last few days, I have seen love expressed in many different ways by mothers. For example, there is the mother who loves her son enough to know that he is different and to allow him to express that difference; the boy has not turned out as his family had expected, even demanded. Then there is a mother who, even though she was scarred by her upbringing, is able (with much forgiveness on the part of her family) to give her four children a love that reveals something of the Ultimate Love. Still another mother told me, "John is falling apart. Hold onto him. Help me." She loves with an almost fierce animal love that has held together her son and her whole family.

Finally there is Mary, the mother of Jesus. Mary recognized her son's uniqueness and nurtured it with love. She saw her son through the difficulties of finding his place in life; endured the anguish of seeing her friends and neighbors reject him; and, ultimately, shared in the awful agony of his death. Through the centuries, Mary has been honored because of her love for her son,

Jesus. Through her, many have come to know God's boundless love.

Although some may question the value of motherhood in today's world of extraordinary change, one has only to look at the mothers he knows to see abiding love made manifest. Think of a mother—yours or any other—whom you love and respect. Enter imaginatively into the life of that mother and her child. Enter into the relationship that is the most creative, the most costly, the most satisfying and enduring of all human relationships. Give thanks, my friends, for mothers and for the family.

Faithfully yours,

Charles Martin

Heavenly Father, Thou hast created us with body and mind and soul, in a complex and mysterious unity of being; grant that we may learn to care for ourselves physically, mentally, and spiritually, remembering that neglect of any part of our nature endangers the health that is your will for all your children.

This we ask in the name of Him who came to bring life in all its abundant wholeness, Jesus Christ Thy Son. Amen.

Robert Cain

XLIV

On Not Getting Sick

January 25, 1977

Dear Friends,

Lately in the news we have been hearing much about the pros and cons of flu shots, and—with winter far from over—we will no doubt hear more. I am certainly in favor of flu shots and other means of preventing illness, but I am even more in favor of not getting sick. As I often tell the boys and the faculty, partly in jest and partly in earnest, "I'm against getting sick! It's unhealthy." Health is maintained not by shots or by medicines alone; it is maintained by taking care of oneself, by practicing wiser living habits than many of us do, and by maintaining a positive outlook on life.

On St. Luke's Day (you will remember that St. Luke is called "the beloved physician"), we usually have a chapel service at which we remember doctors and others engaged in the healing arts. This year I asked our School physician to read that great passage from the Apocrypha about physicians. It contains some magnificent verses: "Honor a physician . . . for the Lord hath created him." "For of the most high cometh healing, and he [the physician] shall receive honor of the king." "Give place to the physician . . . for thou hast need of him." I also asked an alumnus who is considering studying medicine to speak to us. This boy is a paraplegic, crippled by an accident that befell him when he was a Sixth Former; he has had prolonged experience with doctors.

Our alumnus spoke, but from a point of view quite different from that I had expected. He had often expressed to me the need for those engaged in the healing arts to be well-versed in music, art, literature, religion, and interpersonal relationships that they might treat both the disease and the patient. I expected him to develop these ideas. Instead, he spoke of a philosophy of healing and living practiced by some of today's young people. This philosophy seems to have grown out of Oriental religions, contemporary psychology, and a deep feeling of oneness with nature. Its emphasis is on natural foods, simple living, and a reverence for all forms of life as a way to health of body, mind, and spirit. In my youth such thinking was called "living in tune with the infinite"; it found its expression in a great healing movement of the time. Our alumnus said what I firmly believe: we cannot depend upon doctors and science to keep us healthy. We must so live that we keep ourselves healthy.

Some months ago, an article in *The Wall Street Journal* reflected the current thinking of medical experts, expressing with great thoroughness and conviction much the same idea. In the article, Dr. John H. Knowles, President of the research-oriented Rockefeller Foundation, was quoted as saying, "Many Americans have come to look on sloth, gluttony, alcoholic intemperance, reckless driving, sexual frenzy, and smoking as constitutional rights, and they have come to expect government financed cures for all the unhappy consequences." While medical science expects to find dramatic cures for some of today's "common killers," real progress in overcoming these diseases will not be found in cures but in preventative medicine and in wiser living habits.

I have learned from long experience and from a daily examination of the School's absentee and excuse list that good health among boys depends largely upon a proper amount of sleep, a good diet, plenty of exercise, and—most important—upon a healthy attitude toward life. To put it another way, I know that the Deadly Sins of which Dr. Knowles spoke must be replaced by the Cardinal Virtues. And that is quite a job!

The Gospel appointed for Thanksgiving reminds us of another difficult job—not to be anxious. "Which of you, by being anxious, can add one cubit unto the measure of his life?" In addition, it reminds us to make clear our priorities, "Seek ye first the Kingdom of God and his righteousness."

That Gospel was much on my mind through several experiences I had this morning. On the absentee list that came to me early in the morning were several familiar names. One was the name of a boy absent every time he has a slight cold and often when he fears he might catch one from someone else. The argument that the way to health is to ignore slight colds and to take them as part of life is convincing neither to him nor to this parents. Among the excuses from athletics was another familiar name. This boy does not enjoy athletics and that is understandable; not all of us are made for vigorous exercise. Less understandable, however, is the fact that neither he nor his parents believe that his health would improve and his outlook on life would be healthier if he ceased to deceive himself by believing he is unwell and unable to exercise.

Later that morning, a father stopped to see me about the wisdom of his son's continuing to take athletics, since he was having difficulty in his studies. He left understanding, I hope, that the boy has gifts in sports and that his success in sports makes for success in academics. To be whole and healthy, one has to develop his gifts, whatever they may be. What goals one sets, what one believes, how one cares for one's body—these spell the difference between a worried, frustrated life and a healthy, fulfilled one.

It is a fact of life that at times we have to "play hurt." We are not always in excellent health physically, mentally, or emotionally. At times we must carry on when we don't feel good, when we are bearing great burdens, when our lives are not going well. At times this truth is made evident to us with great clarity when we witness someone who is bearing a physical handicap or a personal problem with a grace that has made him or her a finer person than the rest of us.

Finally, although a bit of stoicism may be helpful and the right view of life is important, what is ultimately essential to good health is to be a part of a community committed to health of body, mind, and spirit. Such a community is the Church, in which dwells the Spirit of the Teacher, a Spirit that holds high certain values of healthful living. We have need of doctors—doctors of the mind, body, and spirit—but we have a greater need to remember that the first responsibility for our health lies within ourselves.

Faithfully yours,

Charles Martin

Charles Martin in 1977, on the eve of his retirement as Headmaster.

The Church gives the priest-headmaster and his School the task of bringing one to the other. God's absolute perfection and holiness must be related in mercy to the humblest and proudest child.

Let us thank God for a headmaster and a School that constantly strive to fulfill this vocation.

Let us thank God for a headmaster and a School that are pastors, constantly ministering to those in need; that provide a warm, loving environment; that have challenged the Church and the secular world with the radical demands of the Gospel; that have contributed fine servants and leaders to Church and state.

The Lord is glorious in His saints. O come, let us adore Him.

*The Reverend Craig Eder**

---

*Prayer offered by The Reverend Eder at Canon Martin's farewell service in the Washington Cathedral.

XLV

Farewell

May 25, 1977

Dear Friends,

Ever since I made the decision to retire, I have had in mind a final parent letter. Through it I hoped that I could communicate what I had learned in my twenty-eight years of headmastering at St. Albans and that I could also express my appreciation to all of you.

The most important lesson I have learned as headmaster of St. Albans is how little I know. I don't mean know about all the chores of headmastering, from making schedules and budgets to maintaining buildings and raising money, as important as these matters may be. I mean *know* about the fundamental business of headmastering: understanding people—how they grow, how they learn, how to help them. Such knowledge may come easily to some, but not to me. I still find myself prone to make snap judgments about certain boys—even when I know little about them. Only the pain of past mistakes causes me to stop and dig more deeply for answers.

A parent came to see me this week, troubled because his son was changing from a happy, easygoing boy into a troubled, frustrated one. I was tempted to take the easy route, accepting the words of one master who believed the boy should go to another school. Only after the master and I had met at length, only after I had talked with some of his friends, reviewed his folder, and conferred with other masters, did we begin to discern some answers. And they are not simple ones. How can we help these parents relieve the pressures they are unconsciously putting on their boy, how can we fill the blank spots from his past schooling, how can we find and nurture the boy's strengths and give him confidence—these are difficult tasks. But that is good. I learned again, and I hope the master learned, how little any of us really knows. And that is the beginning of wisdom.

Knowing how little I know has brought special difficulties, particularly in areas about which I thought I knew the most. There was a time when without any doubt I was convinced I knew what was right and what was wrong on almost any given moral question. Problems of cheating, lying, sex, marital relationships, and even problems of relations between nations were moral problems that had for me a very evident right and wrong. That time no longer is, thanks somehow to St. Albans. While I know we must have certainties and must make judgments, I find it increasingly difficult to discern the certainties and even more difficult to base judgments on them. In this I am comforted by the words of the Teacher who had unique understandings of life and who said, "Search and you shall find, knock and it shall be opened, ask and it shall be given you." I am confident that, as I act in the spirit of the Teacher and with much searching, knocking, and asking, I shall come to some reasonable understandings and right answers. At least I have come to know one certainty: when I am most sure I am right, I can be certain I am wrong.

In the months since I announced my resignation, I have had unusual opportunities to learn of much that has been right and much that has been wrong in my years at the School. Opportunities have come from a flood of letters, from alumni meetings, from talks with recent graduates (whose college terms these days seem to give them plenty of time for visiting). One thing above all others we seem to have done right is to insist that our boys learn how to write a structurally sound, clear sentence, or in the words of one of our English masters, Mr. Ruge, to write "clear, correct, reasonably graceful English." From alumni who are lawyers, I have learned over and over again, "Keep on teaching the boys to write." Alumni in the military have said the same, as have alumni now in college. From my own experience with the difficulty of saying clearly what I mean to say, I am convinced that *written* English—not just "English"—should be at the center of any school's curriculum. I wasn't always so sure, but I have learned.

I do not mean to deny the place of math and science, languages and history, art and music in the curriculum. These disciplines are expressions of the richness of human experience. As I write, I think of alumni who are in the foreign service because of Russian courses, professional artists who are painting because of art courses, research scientists who speak gratefully of their math and science courses, musicians whose talents blossomed because of interests developed in the School, and alumni who are pursuing careers in the theater because of their experiences here. The richer the curriculum, the greater the opportunity for a student to develop his interests and unique gifts. A valuable lesson that I have learned as headmaster is that only as a student expresses his uniqueness in the pursuit of a certain academic subject, or in art, or music, or dramatics, or athletics will he grow and do well in those studies for which he has no special aptitude.

Despite all its richness and variety, such a curriculum is still not the basis of a sound education. Inevitably in conversations with alumni I hear, "the master who shaped my life," "the man who meant the most to me." This man might have been a coach, a dorm master, a classroom teacher, or even one known by the pejorative term "administrator." What a diverse group of men our masters are! Yet they have one characteristic in common—they care. And caring, I have come to believe, is the ultimate value in life. Some masters are eccentric, some prickly, some just plain difficult to get along with. But it has been good to work and live with them because they cared about boys. It took me some time to learn this lesson.

The former master who rises up in the mind of an alumnus with affection and gratitude always does so in a context: the time he kicked me out of class, the way he worked us in football, the amount of time he spent helping me understand quadratics, the occasion when he helped me out of a jam. Experiences that seem of no consequence to the master and may be quickly forgotten by him are often highlights in the student's life. Hard work, love of a subject, good sportsmanship, understanding, and warmth—these qualities somehow reveal to the boy what is important to the master and to the School; they touch his sensitivities to the quick. An alumnus once wrote to me, "For nine years, while my family life was undergoing drastic changes, St. Albans was the bedrock constant of my existence."

It may seem that with all I say I have learned about headmastering I am contradicting what I wrote earlier in this letter about my continuing need to search, to seek, and to knock. Not so. There are too many vivid, painful memories of mistakes. Even though, during the past months I have received many letters that have expressed appreciation for St. Albans and its retiring headmaster, I think of the letters I did not receive—particularly from boys who had no reason to express appreciation for their years at St. Albans. There were those who suffered from my mistakes, those for whom the School did not answer needs. And that causes me pain. Thus, the need for searching will ever be with me.

* * * * * *

On Sunday afternoon, May 8, my friend and colleague, Ferdinand Ruge—who had been at St. Albans for more years than I have—died suddenly of a massive heart attack. We had a great memorial service for Mr. Ruge in the Cathedral the following Wednesday. Hundreds of his friends and students were present. Together we gave thanks for all that he had meant to us and to many others. The service was at once sad, deeply moving, and very joyous.

Several times in the weeks before he died, Mr. Ruge had urged me to write a letter in which I would say goodbye to the School family. He would say, "I would be sorry not to receive a farewell letter, and I think others would be, too." I hesitated because I don't like to say goodbye. My emotions are always too close to the surface. Besides, the Martins will be living nearby. Though I shall, of course, remain away from the School—save as I can be helpful—I hope to continue to see my friends in whatever new work will be mine.

I wrote this Parent Letter some weeks ago. It was meant to be not a goodbye but an expression of thanks for all my years at St. Albans. Like everything else I have written, this letter was given to Mr. Ruge for criticism. It came back with as much red ink as the paper of a Fourth Former. As always, we discussed—even argued over—changes of phrase and construction. For the most part, Mr. Ruge's views prevailed. Over the years, his suggestions have helped me to express myself more clearly. I learned much at St. Albans. From no one did I learn more than from Mr. Ruge. This letter is, in a sense, both from him and from me.

In his first letter to the Corinthians, St. Paul says, "If I speak with the tongues of men and angels, and have not love [caring], I am become as sounding brass or a tinkling cymbal. And though I have the gift of prophecy and understand all mysteries and have not love, I am nothing. Love suffereth long, and is kind; love envieth not . . . is not puffed up . . . is not easily provoked . . . rejoiceth in the truth. Love never faileth . . . prophecies, they shall fail; knowledge, it shall vanish away . . . . And now abideth faith, hope, love, these three; but the greatest of these is love." Such love is not soft and sentimental; it is love that searches for truth and understanding. That kind of love is at the very heart of good teaching and good headmastering. For having learned that, I am deeply grateful.

And so to that Teacher, the nature of whose love and caring St. Paul is trying to describe, I give thanks. I give thanks to Him for the students, faculty, parents, and all the members of the St. Albans family from whom I have learned so much in the past twenty-eight years. They will, I believe, help me to learn as I move on to the next phase of my life. So for you, I wish you may continue to learn, to be given occasional glimpses of, and to develop an ever closer relationship with the Teacher who is perfect caring, perfect love, Jesus Christ, Our Lord.

Faithfully yours,

Charles Martin

Sabbatical Excerpts

March 1965—September 1965

The Virgin Islands

The Virgin Islands have a beauty and a charm different from anything I have encountered previously. Small, quaint towns are nestled around the harbors and, in the case of St. Thomas, chiseled into the hillsides. Gaily painted, the houses—tiny for the most part—are crowded upon one another; they reflect the architectural influences of the many countries that have owned the islands throughout their long history. I do not expect to see anything, anywhere, more dramatically beautiful than the ocean, with its ever-changing blues and greens as seen from the highest point on rugged, volcanic St. Thomas. Hot though it was, I never tired of wandering through the winding streets and around the palm-studded countryside of each of the islands. As always, though, the people interested me most.

* * * * *

I visited the wharves and shops of St. Thomas. They were crowded not with natives but with tourists disgorged from the cruise ships and from a steady stream of airplanes. I saw less simplicity and more artificiality there, less beauty and more ugliness. One wonders whether the ordered security and beauty of the simpler life, rooted in an ultimate reality that the islanders apprehend, can survive in a complex, chaotic urban life where order and security are notably lacking and ultimates are difficult to recognize. This is not solely a problem for St. Thomas; it is a problem for us as well.

Rome and Greece

I have missed seeing and being with you; I have missed carrying out all the duties that make up the life of a headmaster. I must admit that I feel somewhat distanced from events that have been occurring in America, and I am sorry not to be sharing in the troubled experiences of my country as they are happening. It is one thing to learn of events a few weeks after they have taken place. It is quite another thing to know them firsthand as they occur.

* * * * *

The climax of my sightseeing tour of Rome and one of the greatest experiences of my life was visiting St. Peter's Church. Time after time I went back to stand before the *Pieta* and to know the exaltation that is in the glory and grandeur of that whole great church. I attended an early service, knelt at the side altars, and even joined in the devotion of the multitudes who, through the centuries, have worn away the toe of St. Peter.

* * * * *

On the day the Russian cosmonaut swam in space, I wandered through the markets at the foot of the Acropolis, partly observing the sights, partly lost in thought about the wonders of outer space. Finally, I came to a kiosk on which was displayed an enormous picture of the Russian cosmonaut feeling his way tentatively out into space. Above me was the Parthenon and an ancient way of life; before me was the astounding picture of the cosmonaut and a new way of life. I stood in awe and was troubled. How can one come to find abiding values in the midst of such starkly contrasting changes? Although I have no ready answer, I do know that as we live and work within the family of man, we uncover or have revealed to us truths that give joy and meaning to all we undertake and that enable us to live with conviction.

* * * * *

One evening I had dinner in Greece with a group of young men who are restless, searching, and quixotic. I suppose one could call them Angry Young Men. Having left the lands of their birth and rearing, they are rootless. Each is alienated from his culture and, to a degree, from himself. With desperate earnestness, each is searching for his identity, for values, for something to give meaning to life. We ate and talked at length; I listened at length. Then, early for them, late for me, I excused myself because of an early church service the next morning.

England

St. Albans School* was my first stop in England. The new headmaster met me at the train with his two children and dog. While we had many talks during the weekend I was there, the subjects were not always serious educational ones. I spent much time with the ten-year-old Kilvington, trying to help him understand American football.

I frequently saw members of the St. Albans School family while I was in England. For example, one alumnus risked his life by riding with me as, for the first time, I drove a left-handed gear-

*St. Albans' British counterpart, located in St. Albans, England.

shift car on the left side of the road in weather that included rain, hail, and some snow.

* * * * *

I love the English countryside. It is so lush and green; the gardens are lovely and the lawns so endless; the villages with cottages gathered around the old parish churches are so picturesque. Occasionally the smallness of the countryside has made me want to draw a deep breath and burst out of it all, or I have wanted to get into a countryside free of people. But where in the world can one be—even at home—where one does not wish to make changes?

* * * * *

At Abingdon College I was shown about by a prefect. His chief interest was history, and there was no doubt of his ability in that field. But he had an equal interest in sports and in the general life of the school. In response to my question as to what meant the most to him at school, he replied (after considerable deliberation), "Learning to stand on my own two feet." It was evident that he was firmly planted on his own two feet at Abingdon and would be at university and in life. Through learning to live with others in the school community, through taking responsibility for himself and for others, as well as through the development of his gifts, he had gained a poise, self-confidence, and healthy maturity that would have done any parent or schoolmaster's heart proud.

* * * * *

London is one of my favorite cities. I had been there long ago and had feared the changes I expected to see, but these were largely superficial. I stood again on the Embankment, thrilled at the sight and sound of Big Ben and at the sight of the Houses of Parliament, the Great Hall, and the Abbey. Occasionally in London I missed an amenity taken for granted at home. I looked with amazement at the Rube Goldberg contraptions that provided hot water or smiled as I got into a hot tub to warm myself at the end of May. But this was just different enough to remind me that I was at another home and not my own.

East Germany

In East Berlin, where one might have expected hostility towards an American clergyman, I was greeted with smiles and courtesy. When the driver of a tram could not change a large bill for me, he waved me on to the trolley for a free ride, and a number of men waiting in line for a taxi insisted on putting me at the head.

Japan

The Diocese of Tokyo is no small one! It is a city of 11,000,000 people, people who are everywhere in great numbers. Imagine a Christmas rush in downtown Washington. Double that and you have some idea of the restless, surging crowds in downtown Tokyo on any evening of the year. Imagine a city so big that taxi drivers do not know their way around, a city completely unplanned, with twisting alleys and paths for streets, without benefit of street names or numbers. Tokyo is, in short, no pleasant place to live; yet, it is a thrilling city, filled with dynamic, throbbing life and color.

* * * * *

The countryside of Japan is very different from the turbulent city. While there are none of the confusions and noises of the city in these rural areas, one is always aware of the same intense, constant energy that is found in Tokyo and that *is* the Japanese people. This restless energy is apparent in the farmers and in the busy life of the villages. There is activity in the midst of serenity as these energetic, intense people reclaim, redeem, and make do. The scene may change, but the people do not. Their presence and its effect give a common identity both to the country and the city.

* * * * *

I have just completed the most thrilling part of my leave—returning home. I have seen many wonderful people in many strange and interesting parts of the world, and I have had one of the most valuable experiences of my life. But still, nothing in the experience matched the thrill of finally getting home! America looks more lovely by far today than it had before I left. And my family (I'd always thought they were a rather decent lot) has improved extraordinarily while I was away! To my larger family, St. Albans . . . my, it's good to be back among you. To walk on the Close, to step into my study, to walk through the buildings and down to the fields, to see and greet boys and colleagues, was to return to paradise. All of which is to say that I have had a very valuable and interesting experience, proven—if proof be necessary—by the great joy of getting back home.

School Life—Selected Excerpts

(1950–1977)

Cleopatra—1950*

One tragedy marred our family's summer vacation. Our family dog, Cleopatra, died. We had been in Vermont only a short time when she became ill and quietly slipped out. Her heart refused to continue its labor. It hurt to have her go, but we gave thanks to the good Lord for eleven years of her gentle, devoted companionship.

Now there is a new Cleo—Cleopatra II. She is fawn colored and, at three months, a fraction of the size of Cleo I. She cannot wag her tail (for she doesn't have much of a tail), but she can wiggle her whole body in greeting. Although she will not be able to take Cleo I's place in our affections, perhaps she can make a very real place of her own.

---

*Notes concerning the history of Charles Martin's bulldogs: He recalls, "In about 1934, while I was attending a football game at Episcopal Academy, a lady with a bulldog on a leash approached me. She asked whether I would like to have the dog, and I said, 'yes.' The dog was already named Cleopatra. From that time on, I have had six bulldogs—five females (Cleopatras) and one male (Mark Anthony). The lifespan of a bulldog is relatively short—about eight or ten years. When I came to St. Albans, the School had no mascot; the football team was then called the St. Albans Saints. After I arrived, the bulldog became our mascot, and the name, the St. Albans Bulldogs, has remained ever since.

Starting of School—1951

This has not been a quiet summer at School. Plasterers, painters, carpenters, and brick masons have made the air heavy with dust and odors, stormy with noise and activity. From this activity comes an immediately startling change—a huge fire escape attached to the rear of our main building. Somewhat camouflaged but still plainly visible, it seems large enough to evacuate the Pentagon. Less noticeable but still plainly visible are three newly fireproofed stairways, with multitudinous doors, passageways, and exit lights. We wanted to make the School completely modern in terms of fire protection. Many times I have been heavy of heart at the decision, sometimes because of the fearsome cost, always at the changes that threatened the character of the building. I must now admit that my worry was—like most worry—unjustified.

The Student Stoop—1953

I run what amounts to a one-man campaign throughout the School year against the "student stoop." Finding that words do not help much, I go about the halls, classrooms, and dining room straightening up boys, pushing their chests from their backs to where chests ought to be, pulling shoulders back, and generally being a back thumper. I would be grateful if by word and example all of us would become more conscious of the very bad posture of our boys. Together, and with the possible aid of posture classes, I hope we can improve the situation. The strange posture that is so common may be a tribute to the studious habits of our boys, but I doubt it. Instead, I would like our boys to keep the studious habits but to face the world with chins up, chests out, and stomachs in.

Vacation's End—1954

The summer vacation is at an end. And thank the good Lord for that! Vacation is very welcome when it comes, but for most of us who are associated with the School—boy, parent, and master—it is good when vacation is over. I shall be glad to get back into the regular routine of things. At the moment, the buildings seem lifeless and forbidding. I will be glad to see them come alive again, even though the activity of the School year may at times become strenuous. It is not from boredom that it will be good to get back into the routine, but it will simply be good to see everyone again and to feel that one is back in the normal workings of life.

Gossip—1956

"Gossip" is an ugly word. At least it has always seemed so to me until a few days ago when I read a delightful informal essay in defense of gossip—not, of course, about the malicious type so frequently associated with the word—but about good gossip. Gossip is news that relates to people. If we are interested in people, then we will naturally want and need news of them. Moreover, gossip is more desirable than preaching, exhortation, or general advice. It gets away from the abstract and down to the concrete; thus it has greater saving power. It is of the earth—a very natural and necessary part of life.

Centennial—1959

In a sense, our School is not fifty years old, nor are we dependent on our own wisdom to meet the opportunities before us. We are centuries old, and our wisdom is of a life that has come through the centuries. Our life goes back to a young man named

Alban, who lived 1500 years ago in Britain. Well born and well educated, Alban had an open-mindedness that enabled him to understand new ideas and to see in the Teacher called Jesus Christ that which most of his contemporaries were unable to see. More, he had the courage to hold to what he saw and believed in the midst of misunderstanding and hatred—even unto death. The life of Alban, or the understandings of the life of the Teacher that were in Alban, lived on after his death. The hill on which he was executed was named after him, and on that hill a cathedral and a school were built so that the life that was in him might be honored and continued. Fifteen hundred years later on a hill, the highest spot in Washington—named in honor of Alban—our School came into being that boys might continue to know the life of the Teacher who lived in Alban.

In the confidence of fifty years of good life, in the confidence and in the spirit of Him who has lived through the years, we face the future with courage and good cheer.

Mr. Ruge—1960

Mr. Ruge has an office, but it is only a place where he puts his hat and from which he departs. His place of work is in the hall as he grabs a boy, at the emergency into which he plunges madly, in the Sitting Room with an alumnus whom he entertains or counsels. I know the reason for the devotion of people to Mr. Ruge. It's simple. He gives himself to everyone and everything at St. Albans with unstinting intensity.

Starting of School—1961

Yesterday I came over to my office. It had an unnaturally spick-and-span look. Everything was in place—no boys, no dogs, nobody around. As a result, I couldn't locate anything.

Today there's noise around. But it is good noise. There's the noise of the kitchen and of the waxing machine in the Common Room, the noise of men shouting as they move furniture, of a group of alumni saying goodbye to a faculty member, of a boy asking, "Where's the Canon?" These are the noises of School making ready to open. These are the sounds of life, giving purpose and meaning to *my* life. It is good to hear them.

Vermont—1963

My family and I have just returned from Vermont. The state has never seemed so lovely. To climb the mountain trails was to know new strength; to fish on the lake was to know quiet and peace. Man needs more of nature with its beauty, with its quietness and grandeur undisturbed. Man and nature are of one piece. As man despoils nature, he weakens his own life and becomes prey to the plagues of modernity—rootlessness, restlessness, lostness. It was good to be in Vermont, and the full measure of that goodness is in the satisfaction of coming home.

Learning—1964

"Sing. Get your voice up there. Use your muscles, exercise them. Singing is not an intellectual exercise; it is physical exercise. Sing!" cried our choir master to the boys of the Upper School in chapel as he tried to stop them from growling. The boys sang well; they have been singing better in chapel ever since. The idea that singing is physical exercise might not have been new to the boys, but somehow the idea caught their imaginations, and ever since then they have been singing as never before.

We have all had this kind of experience. We work away at something, but we fail to understand it. Then something happens and suddenly all becomes clear; we wonder how we could have been so stupid. We pass a tree day after day and fail to see it, or we see it only as another tree. Suddenly our eyes are opened, and we see it in all its uniqueness and beauty. We wonder where our eyes have been. We live with our boy, believing that we know him reasonably well. Then we have an experience—Could this be *our* boy? And from that day forward, we know our son differently.

Significant learning, flashes of insight, new understandings come as we are able to lay aside familiar patterns of thought, habits of behaving, structures and rigidities of living—in short, they come only as we are able to change and to grow. Education is liberation from the bonds that inhibit growth.

Religious Change—1964

The winds of change are violent in religion. The Vatican Council, the visit of the Pope to the Holy Land, the Anglican Congress, the thinking of the Bishop as he expresses it in a book, *Honest to God*, are evidence of changes greater than Western Civilization has known since the Reformation. At School we are all trying to open ourselves to these changes, to liberate our minds, to comprehend what is happening. To whatever degree we are able to do this—and we do not fool ourselves; we know that human growth is slow—we shall see God in the world differently and so all life for us will, I hope, become different and new.

Honors and Achievements—1965

As I write of honors and strengths, I am mindful of those to whom honors have not come, of those whose strengths are not at once apparent, and of those who have had a larger share of difficulty than most. It is interesting to observe that for those individuals who seemed not to excel early in their lives, life later has a way of raising them up to places of success and high distinction. We can be proud and confident about all of our boys and of their promise in life.

Life's Certainties—1965

There may be many uncertainties in life, but there are also many certainties. The kindness, courtesy, and understanding of friends; the joy, affection, and love of homes; the naturalness, spontaneity, and hope of children; the striving, achievement, and satisfaction of work. In these I trust; in these I believe; in these I have confidence. I may not always know or recognize the form in which they are expressed, but I know they exist, and I know that in them is that which is good, fine, and noble. And I know them to have been incarnate in a Teacher in whom I can trust.

We Have Changed—1966

Over the years our School has changed. No longer are we an academic institution on a hill isolated from the rest of the world, providing a traditional education to a privileged few. We are now a School that in the normal academic year gives what I hope is a top-notch education to boys from many parts of the country and even of the world. No longer living largely to ourselves, we have relations with public, parochial, and other independent schools, as well as with a number of community agencies. All of this is to the great profit of our own boys and to the usefulness of other young people and the community at large.

Long Hair—1968

Many people get so upset about the length of hair that, at the beginning of the year, it may be helpful to parents for me to offer my own thinking on the matter. I prefer short hair because I'm used to it. Furthermore, short hair, neatly cared for, tends to give a boy a clean-cut, alert appearance—the appearance of one who is ready and competent to take on the world.

However, I do not become grievously upset at reasonably long hair. Styles change, I know. Our family album shows some old gentlemen (and some younger ones, too) sporting beards, sideburns, mutton chops, and other old-fashioned, tonsorial adornments. On the mantlepiece in my study is a small bust of Ben Franklin with long curls. At St. Albans, we would prefer to avoid extremes, if possible.

What is extreme I choose not to define. I take it for granted that parents have some judgment and control, that boys have more wisdom and judgment than most of us give them credit for. I will expect parents and boys to use their own discretion. When nudging is necessary, I will depend upon the masters in charge of discipline to exert it.

But let us not get hung up on the subject of long hair. If we are going to be concerned about aberrations of appearance, let it be about what those aberrations often symbolize—boys who are sensitive, insecure, troubled, unable or unwilling to adjust to a life they cannot comprehend or in which they cannot find a meaningful place. Our job at St. Albans is to give boys that security, to give their lives a purpose and meaning that will enable them to cope with the world as it is and the wisdom and vision to help move it in a healthier direction.

To Teach Less and Learn More—1968

I am convinced that we cannot educate boys simply by demanding that they learn more and more. We must not simply add subjects to our curriculum and lengthen our working day. There is already too much pressure on young people, and their days are already too long—longer by far than their parents' working days. Our boys need more leisure, more time to reflect, more time to develop individuality. We need to teach less and learn more, to memorize less and to think more.

Chapel—1969

My own convictions about chapel are strong. To me there is a place for a regular coming-together of the School community to bring our concerns, achievements, and failures as well as our anxieties and joys before the highest that we know, Him who transcends all. The job is to learn how we can do so more effectively in today's world.

Past and Future—1969

We all love the old; we all love that in which our life is deeply rooted. This is even more true today because so little seems to remain unchanged. And that is right. It is natural for us to hold tenaciously and emotionally to the past, not quite as natural for us to move purposefully into the future. Yet we know we must, and indeed we are proud when we do. I hope at St. Albans that we can always hold to that which is abiding and good in the past, yet always have the courage and the imagination to move confidently into the future.

In striving to hold onto the values of the past and at the same time face the new, let us remember our men in Vietnam. We are so busy with our own concerns that it is easy for us to forget those alumni and the 500,000 others now serving in Vietnam. I receive many letters from young graduates as they agonize over what they should do. Can they kill? Can they participate in this war? Should they go to jail? It is never easy to hold on to the abiding and the good while moving into an uncertain future in a time of radical change.

To be unaware of or simply to ignore the tragedy of the war in Asia is not only to fail to understand and to share in the hurt of people, but also to be coarsened and hardened inwardly. By imaginative and sensitive concern and with whatever good works possible, we must seek to enter into the life of the people of Vietnam and of our soldiers who are working, living, and dying there.

Moon Landing—1969

With you and most of the world, I was fixed before the television screen as the Lunar Module hovered over the moon, inching its way along and finally landing. The slow, hesitant descent of Neil Armstrong's foot, its tentative placement on the moon, and then Armstrong's triumphant words, "One small step for man, one giant leap for mankind," left me completely exhausted. Until the television screen darkened and the telecast ended, time ceased, and I lived an eternity. The world had witnessed a miracle.

The older of us in the School family knew a miracle in the moon landing: the moon made of green cheese, the moon that the cow jumped over, the moon that the poets sang about and in whose pale, silvery light we spent so much of our life will never be the same to any of us. For most of our boys in School what happened was not so much a miracle as a straightforward achievement of modern technology. And, I suppose, for some of the youngest what they experienced was expressed by a cartoon in *The New Yorker* that pictured a family seated before the television, all, save the youngest, watching in awe the pictures of the moon surface transmitted by Telstar. The youngest was complaining, "We saw that before; let's turn to something else." There may or may not be a generation gap between us, but there are certainly differences of seeing and understanding life. It is important for us to recall this fact as we observe young people and their music, films, hair, drugs, demonstrations, and Woodstock festivals . . . .

The Church—1973

Waiting in the Cathedral for a funeral service to begin, I drifted off into a sea of memories. With new clarity I understood how I had been nurtured in the Church, how my values had been formed, how my life had been shaped. And I was grateful. I thought of our boys and coveted for them the experience I have had in the Church—but they can never have it. The times in which we live deny them that. Young people cannot know the richness of Church life that gave my generation standards to live by and understandings that made life good.

Young people are not part of the Church as past generations were, for the Church does not meet their needs. It is troubled, and, like all institutions, changing. Yet young people's need for standards, purpose, meaning, and faith is perhaps more desperate today than it was for those of us who grew up during a more stable era. My mood was deepening until I reminded myself that St. Albans is part of the Church, a significant part for those who share in its life. We are a community in which young people are growing, finding themselves, discovering their places in life. They are being given a heritage different from that of an earlier generation, yet in some ways the same. Though experiences differ, the spirit and essential life are the same. The true and the right are not as clear today as we believed them to be in the past, but searching and openness to know the true and the right seem to be more evident today than they were in the past. I was lifted out of my reverie by the Dean of the Cathedral saying, "I am the resurrection and the life saith the Lord; he that believeth in me shall never die."

The Unexpected—1975

A beautiful day, a lovely trip, and an exciting football game—these experiences grew out of a most unpromising day. And I believe that, in a nutshell, is life. It is the unpromising that often becomes promising, the difficult that often becomes most rewarding, the hard and the painful that often reveal the true, the beautiful, and the good.

Summer—1976

So much of significance has happened so quickly that when I think back over the summer, it seems as though the last days of school were years ago. I suppose every summer is filled with special events, but surely this one held more than the usual.

There was the glorious Fourth of July celebration of the 200th anniversary of our nation's birth with its Tall Ships, dazzling fireworks, bell ringing, and services of thanksgiving. It was a day when America cast off the pain and hurt of the last decade, laid aside heavy self-doubts, and knew again the self-confidence and the renewed sense of purpose that have been among the great strengths of our nation. To use a current phrase, we have been "born again" as we enter into our third century of life.

The Democratic Convention was quiet and predictable, yet very moving at the end. To me, it was more than a political convention. It was an event that marked the end of confrontation and the beginning of a new civility and a common concern—not in politics alone but in our daily life as well.

Then there were the Olympics. I enjoyed the competitions, although I was troubled by the media's constant hammering on such subjects as drugs, commercialism, and political ploys—as if we were in an ideal world where such evils did not exist. Overall, the Olympics offered glimpses of grace and beauty, of heartwarming sportsmanship, and of uplifting triumphs of the human spirit.

Many of us witnessed Viking's flight to Mars. What an awesome event! How can we experience a miracle and take it for granted? Save for an occasional flare of excitement as scientists examined the planet's surface for indications of life, the Viking mission—even with all its technological wonders and its probing of the unknown—evoked little national interest. Perhaps the Viking flight moved me as it did partly because of my visit to the

National Air and Space Museum. I was awed and humbled by that magnificent building, by the artistry of the displays, and by the incredible achievements in aviation and rocketry. I was grateful to have seen these extraordinary accomplishments of man.

As I write, the Republican Convention with all its promise of excitement is in progress. What a summer!

Inauguration—1977

After having urged our boys to attend the Inauguration, I felt obliged to do the same. Jammed, packed, and sardined are inadequate adjectives to describe my first ride in our multi-billion-dollar Metro. The subway was attractive and moved silently and well—when it moved. Fun and gaiety were evident everywhere as we joked, visited with strangers, bought mementos, got cold and warm. After several hours, concerned lest my two-year-old grandchild would lose her good humor, we headed home.

I enjoyed being in the crowd, enjoyed being caught up with everyone else in the celebration that welcomed a new leader, President Carter, and his family. At home, filled with a warm sense of goodwill for our President, we settled before the TV for the remainder of the festivities.

Living in Washington, it is easy for us to take for granted whatever goes on. There are always important people around and significant events occurring. It is easier to sit by passively and to participate vicariously in events on TV than to participate actively. Still, I favor direct involvement. Our boys ushered, gave out programs, set up and cleaned up at the swearing in, helped at the parade and at the balls. It was good for them to join in the celebration of the simple but awesome transfer of governmental power. Our new America can never become a reality if we sit by and do not participate. We all need to make a commitment to give ourselves a better understanding of and a fuller participation in our government that neither a leader nor all our representatives in Washington can make good without the support and active participation of all people—of our boys and of you and me.